SCHOOLYARD
BULLIES

Messing with
British Columbia's
Education System

MIKE CRAWLEY

ORCA BOOK PUBLISHERS

To my parents,
who taught me the values
of fairness and honesty

Canadian Cataloguing in Publication Data
Crawley, Mike, 1968-
  Schoolyard bullies

  Includes bibliographical references and index.
  ISBN 1-55143-043-6
  1. Education and state—British Columbia. 2. Educational change—British Columbia. 3. Education—British Columbia. I. Title.
LA418.B7C72 1995   379.711   C95-910454-2

We gratefully acknowledge the financial support of The Canada Council.

Cover design by Christine Toller
Cover concept by Angèle Beausoleil

Printed and bound in Canada

Orca Book Publishers
P.O. Box 5626, Station B
Victoria, BC Canada
V8R 6S4

10 9 8 7 6 5 4 3 2 1

The education your children deserve, and will demand, requires a revolution in the school system of which you are a product.

— Ivan Illich

Education would certainly be in a decline if the same methods of instruction were being used to teach the pupils of today that were in vogue for teaching their parents.

— Report of the Royal Commission on Education, 1960

ACKNOWLEDGEMENTS

I want to thank everyone who took the time to talk to me during my research for this book, whether in formal interviews or informal chats. There are too many to list individually, but almost all are named in the text—politicians, university professors, ministry staff, superintendents, BCTF representatives, school trustees, principals, teachers, parents, and students. I found nearly all to be forthcoming and I appreciated their insights.

I also had help from staff at the UBC education library and the Vancouver Public Library. A good librarian is a journalist's best friend.

The staff at Orca Book Publishers deserve my thanks, especially Bob Tyrrell, who was enthusiastic about this project from the moment I proposed it to him even though he'd never met me before.

I thank Charles Ungerleider of UBC who gave of his time to read a draft. His suggestions were extremely useful.

Thanks to the friends who gave encouragement through the process and feedback on early versions of the manuscript. They helped in other ways, too: John Balogh put me up in Victoria, Trefor Smith was an intellectually rigorous sounding board for my ideas, and Rob Klovance emphasized the need for good writing. Finally, I thank Joanna Wedge for reading with a critical eye, for believing in me, and for coping with a partner whose mind was absorbed in the education system.

CONTENTS

INTRODUCTION

Ultimately, in the $4-billion-a-year industry that is British Columbia's public school system—from the education minister, down through the bureaucracy, trustees, superintendents, principals, teachers, janitors, the school buildings, the library books, the desks—everything exists for one reason: to provide an education for students. In the end, all the political statements and curriculum guides and professional development workshops boil down to what goes on in the classroom every day, the learning experiences of 600,000 children. While researching this book and while working as a newspaper reporter, I met some of these 600,000 kids. Many were bright, some were troublemakers, some were both. But all share one thing: every one of them has a right to the best public school experience possible. If we as a society don't provide that, we fail. We're the ones who should receive a letter F on our collective report card. It is this guiding philosophy—doing what's best for students—that I tried to keep in mind while researching and writing this book. The kids are one of the reasons this book is important.

It's also important because of the huge role the education system plays in the daily lives of the people in this province. And the

600,000 students and their parents are only part of the story: the financial significance of education also makes it worthy of scrutiny. The 1995–96 education budget is a hair's breadth short of $4 billion, the second biggest item after health care. In perspective, the latest gross domestic product figures (1993) for B.C.'s biggest industries show lumber pumps $2.94 billion into the provincial economy, tourism $2.76 billion, forestry $2.74 billion, residential construction $2.4 billion, and mining $1.7 billion. Education (counting post-secondary) employed 111,000 people in 1993, as many as the low-paying accommodation and food service industry and more than construction (108,000), finance, insurance, and real estate (95,000), and logging, lumber, and pulp and paper (94,000).

Finally, the story of education change in B.C. is important because of the significance of the reforms that have been debated since the Royal Commission report of 1988. This was not mere window-dressing of school curricula, tidying the little red schoolhouse. Educators from around the world were watching. Various people in the system call it the most exciting time in education in their careers. It's been described as the biggest single education reform ever undertaken by an entire jurisdiction in North America.

The story of British Columbia's attempt at education reform is also a good read. As I researched this book, I discovered that it has all the elements of a good novel: intriguing characters, delicious irony, suspense, plot twists, angry shouting matches, political manoeuvring, firings, and an ending that isn't clear-cut. The only difference is that this isn't fiction, it's fact. This is not to say the issues are treated lightly, only to point out that this book is not a dull treatise about an institutional subject. It's a story of real people with honest foibles, battling for a cause they believe in against strong forces in society but doing it in a problematic way. The tale strikes close to home because, ultimately, the ones affected by it are our children.

My biggest objective in telling the story of the education reform process in B.C. is honesty. I come at this with no axes to grind, with no sacred cows, and with no preconceived ideology except one with which everyone should agree: a desire to see the school system do what's best for kids (and by that I mean all kids, not just middle-class kids or bright ones). I want to move beyond rhetoric (like "the Year 2000 lacks standards") to get at the real issues. I don't dismiss the critics or trivialize the criticisms of Year 2000, but I also refuse to accept at face value an outright rejection of its principles. I don't engage in teacher-bashing, but I believe that the practice of teaching needs improvement.

To be as honest as possible means addressing all the complexities of a difficult issue. Education is not like the responsibilities held by other government ministries, such as building highways. You can put a highway here or you can put it there. You can make it four lanes or two lanes. You can expropriate land or divert the route. Plough it in the winter, pave it in the summer. Not to diminish the importance of the Highways Ministry's tasks, but they are far less subtle than teaching more than half a million kids—each one unique—how to read, write, and calculate. Education reform can be as emotional an issue as capital punishment or abortion, but it's even more complex because it's not something on which one can be simply pro or con, it's multi-dimensional. This book tries to deal with all the dimensions and presents the arguments to the reader as fairly as possible.

Yet it's not a book written without passion. I'm thrilled at the things our school system does well, and for that, I praise it, but I won't allow it to ignore the fact that thousands of kids every year drop out. I bristle at the schoolyard bullies of the title: the politicians who use the school system only for political self-interest, the union leaders and bureaucrats who see the education system only in terms of dollars, people inside and outside the system who wax romantic for the golden age of education, when principals blistered kids' palms with leather straps, where teachers droned on endlessly in Latin class, and where only kids who were bound for college or university made it to graduation day.

Don't expect this book to be an apologist for one type of miracle cure education reform. It won't urge you to jump on a new bandwagon. Nor will it cry that our schools are failing and that we must abandon everything we've done until now. There are enough books about education filled with controversial statements, heated admonitions, and cure-all solutions. This book will instead try to be reasonable. I believe that people who honestly care about kids yet argue for opposing views of education can agree on far more things than they differ. Unfortunately, the microscope of public opinion gets focused on the differences and polarization occurs. This book calls for finding the common ground.

THE STORY

In 1988, after the B.C. Royal Commission on Education issued its report, many in the school system expected it would end up gathering dust on the government's shelves. After all, the Royal Commission only took place because Premier Bill Vander Zalm promised it during an election campaign and was obliged to follow through. The province was still limping from the "school wars" waged by the restraint-minded government of Bill Bennett. Cynicism was *de rigueur* among educators.

So when the Social Credit government endorsed all but two of the Royal Commission's eighty-three recommendations, the enthusiasm and excitement in the school system were unprecedented. Even the sceptics were forced to acknowledge that tangible changes were being proposed when the Education Ministry unveiled the framework for the Year 2000 education program, an ambitious strategy for widespread reform.

What's taken place since then is the focus of this book. My goal is to tell the untold story of what happened to Year 2000. Although the reforms attracted plenty of media attention, the behind-the-scenes process has never been laid bare to the public. In doing so, I hope to contribute to a more informed debate about how children are taught in our schools and how education reforms are implemented. This book examines the Royal Commission and the Year 2000 proposals for what they were, it describes the process of putting their recommendations into practice, and it reveals what went wrong.

If the official history of the education reform process in B.C. were being written without this book, it would say that Year 2000 philosophy was flawed, causing a groundswell of public opposition, which prompted the NDP government to kill the program in September 1993. But this book argues that this conventional wisdom is false, leaving out a host of other far more complex factors that led to the government's decision. I'll address them in this introduction under three broad categories—mistakes made by the program's backers, the program's diverse and powerful opponents, and politics.

MISTAKES

At the heart of what went wrong with Year 2000, people in the government either misunderstood how to go about changing as massive and complicated a system as education, or else weren't able to translate their understanding into action. The Education Ministry acted as if issuing documents amid fanfare would be enough to persuade staff in the field of Year 2000's benefits and get them to take action. Issuing curriculum documents only brings about change on paper: bringing about change in practice requires long-term professional development. Also lacking was a sensitivity to the effect that the changes would have on people in the system. The government tried to order teachers to do certain things in their classroom, despite the obvious potential for backlash.

The people in the Education Ministry assigned to carry out the change virtually ignored the need to persuade people outside the education system of its benefits, as if such a politically sensitive reform could proceed without public support. And when they tried to pitch the program to the public, they spoke in educational jargon, sending justifiable fears through parents.

That was part of the poor communication that was pervasive in the education reform process. The people assigned to spell out the vision could not articulate it well, the people in the field who needed to carry it out misunderstood the vision, the leadership in government sent mixed messages of support and criticism.

OPPONENTS

Second, the forces that wanted to keep the status quo in education were massive. What's really interesting is the variety of these groups: the B.C. Teachers' Federation, high-school teachers, universities, and political conservatives.

The opposition of the BCTF was a key factor almost ignored by media observers. In fact, many critics who argued that Year 2000 was too "touchy-feely" thought the BCTF was behind the program. Ostensibly, the BCTF is a union with a social conscience and a left-wing philosophy. In reality, it can be as conservative as any other part of the education establishment. Publicly, BCTF leaders say they couldn't take a stand in favour of Year 2000 because the federation's membership was divided. But this book argues that there was general support for Year 2000 principles among teachers. The excuse that there wasn't consensus is spurious: the union has taken a position on lots of issues completely unrelated to education on which there couldn't have been consensus. Arguably, the real reason for its opposition was politics. The BCTF was simply unwilling to endorse an education reform that came from Social Credit, no matter how well the reform fit into its own philosophy, no matter how good the reform would be for kids.

The most concerted opposition among public school staff came from a segment of secondary-school teachers. Year 2000 proposals would have endangered their identity as subject specialists and eroded some of their turf. This book argues that secondary-school teachers by their very nature are likely to accept the status quo in education because they are successful products of the system.

University academics weighed in against Year 2000 and some of their criticisms were justified. But what's really remarkable is the disproportionate influence of the universities in the debate. A main objective of the school reforms was to better serve the 70 percent of students who don't continue with post-secondary education. This book argues that by bowing to pressure from the universities, the government sent an implicit message that the 30 percent of public school students who take post-secondary education are more important than the rest.

The other main source of opposition came from outside the education system in the form of political conservatives. Although some of the public criticism was not based on ideology, it can be shown that a right-of-centre political philosophy was the common thread linking many of the most vocal public opponents of Year 2000.

POLITICS

The third factor that led the government to announce the failure of Year 2000 was the shift in ideological perspective. Politics is inherent in education, a factor that people in the system ignore at their peril. It's naive to think we can have education without politics. That's why this book spells out political and ideological background to Year 2000 and its opposition. Year 2000 was in its infancy at a time when Canadian politics was beginning to shift toward the right, a trend that first showed itself in the rise in popularity of the Reform party, but which many observers did not see until as recently as June 1995 when the Progressive Conservatives won the Ontario election with a solidly right-wing platform. In this climate, the mistakes of Year 2000 sowed the seeds for a right-wing critique of school, resulting in a demand for charter schools and the popularity of the "traditional" school model, portrayed as the opposite of Year 2000. This was the context in which the NDP decided it was politically expedient to embrace more conservative education tenets, ignoring the Royal Commission's call for meeting the social needs of children.

The official history of education reform says that NDP Premier Mike Harcourt announced the failure of Year 2000 based on widespread opposition in a public opinion poll. But this book reveals that the results of the government-commissioned poll don't totally support the argument. In fact, observers speculate that the public was being hoodwinked by a government that simply wanted to look decisive and wanted to put its own stamp on an education program designed by the previous party in power.

Finally, the "official version" of the past few years in B.C. education also ignores the evidence presented in this book that despite everything that happened to Year 2000—the mistakes of the Education Ministry, the strength of the opposition, and the government's official announcement of its failure—the program is not dead. This is one of the most important conclusions of this book. Many individual teachers, schools, and districts are using Year 2000-type programs and techniques regardless of government policy because they feel that the principles work.

So this means that although many people thought Year 2000 had been laid to rest, the debate is far from over.

A few notes on functional aspects: because this book, by its very nature, needs to be accessible to the general public and so that it doesn't look like an academic text, I've tried to minimize the number of footnotes. My sources are fully referenced in the bibliography. When I quote directly from a document, an endnote is included only when the source isn't mentioned in the text. All other items in quotation marks come from my personal interviews with the subjects, conducted in early 1995.

All references to "the Royal Commission" mean the 1988 British Columbia Royal Commission on Education, headed by the late Barry Sullivan, Q.C.

For the sake of brevity, I use acronyms for frequently cited organizations and institutions in B.C. education. For those unfamiliar with the province, they are—BCTF: B.C. Teachers' Federation; BCSTA: B.C. School Trustees Association; EAC: Education Advisory Council; SFU: Simon Fraser University; UBC: University of British Columbia; U-Vic: University of Victoria.

[1]
THE STATE OF SCHOOLS

On a bright April morning, Kerri Wallin, the principal of Tynehead Montessori School in Surrey, excuses herself to deal with a discipline problem. A skinny blond boy named Michael, who looks about ten, has been sent to the principal's office because of a scuffle on the playground. Wallin confronts Michael with a metal chain and asks why he brought it to school. "It was in my bag," he replies, unwilling to meet her eye. "Look at me, Michael," she admonishes, presenting the chain in her palm like a cold, hard fact. "This is dangerous," she declares.

It turns out that Michael was hitting another boy with the chain, a dog's choke-collar, before classes began. "Spring is in the air," laments Wallin.

This is just one example of the thousands of problems schools throughout B.C. face every day of the year. Violence isn't the only thing. In fact, it's probably more accurate to consider violence as a symptom of a multitude of other problems in society. In a survey the B.C. Teachers' Federation published in 1994, seven out of ten teachers said abuse in the home is a contributing factor to violence in their schools. Among secondary-school teachers, some 70 percent said alcohol and drug abuse played a role in violence, while close to 60 percent attributed it in part to racism.

What do things like this have to do with curriculum reform? Plenty. More than proponents of education reform thought.

So says Olav Slaymaker, an associate vice-president of research at the University of British Columbia. He has a daughter who is a teacher and his wife is a child-care worker. "When I see the circumstances they have to deal with, this whole discussion (of education change) has taken place at a rarified level. The problem is much more deep-seated than tampering with the curriculum. It's a failure of imagination not to see how deeply the social context has changed." He says the public thinks teachers can simply pump children full of knowledge and says the Education Ministry works on the assumption that the children being taught come to school with no baggage or impediments to learning. He urges that society get to the root of the problems by dealing with the impediments.

"Kids know what the real world is all about, believe me," says John O'Fee, a lawyer and chairman of the Kamloops school board. Kids come to school hungry, poor, beaten up. Some kids stay at school longer than they need to because, unlike home, it's a pleasant routine, a place where they're accepted, where people are there for them. They see the teacher as a surrogate parent.

Those are anecdotal perspectives on our changing social context. The Royal Commission on Education examined more thoroughly the various factors that shape British Columbia society and its schools. Among these, three have undergone the most rapid change in the preceding decades and have the most profound impact on the schools of the 1990s: ethnic heritage, family structure, and the economy.

ETHNIC HERITAGE

In 1961, people of non-European heritage made up 6.6 percent of the province's population. By 1991, that percentage had changed to 14.4 percent. The biggest growth comes from Asia. The 1961 census says there were 40,000 Asians in B.C. (24,000 Chinese, 10,000 Japanese, and 4,500 from the Indian subcontinent). In the thirty years since, while the overall population of the province has doubled to 3.2 million from 1.6 million, the Asian population is nine times larger, growing to 371,000 in 1991. Chinese and South Asians are now the third- and fourth-largest ethnic groups in the province, behind British and German. The ethnic diversity is even more profound in the cities: the 1991 census says the greater Vancouver region is home to 467,350 immigrants out of a total population of 1.5 million. And ethnic diversity is greatest amongst the young. For half of the kids in the Vancouver school district, English is not the language spoken at home. Look at almost any urban school and you'll see a kaleidoscope of faces. Inside, many classrooms feature world maps on their bulletin boards with widely scattered push-pins representing the origins of their pupils.

Those are the statistics. The challenge, then, is "insuring appropriate reflection of the diversity without losing sight of the aims of educating for a productive, socially responsible citizenry," said scholar Jorgen Dahle in the Royal Commission report. Our schools must respond to their changing ethnic makeup with teaching that understands the different cultural assumptions of the students and their families.

FAMILY STRUCTURE

It's been said so many times that our society is no longer what it was in the 1950s—with father going off to work and mother staying home to cook and clean and be there for the children when they arrive home from school—that there should be no need to repeat the facts. Yet the actions of some people in our society seem to indicate they've ignored the realities, continuing to operate under the same assumptions of a generation or two ago.

The 1991 census tells the story: 12 percent of all families in B.C. are led by single parents, twice the number of 1961. In 58 percent of couples, both adults are in the labour force. In 1961, that was the case for only 21 percent of couples. The effect is even more profound in certain neighbourhoods and cities, like Vancouver, where more than one-third of all students come from single-parent families.

These two factors alone—the increase in single-parent families and the three-fold jump in the number of families in which both adults work outside the home—have such a profound effect on the children who attend our schools, it's virtually impossible to describe. Pining for the 1950s is pointless. Society has changed and we must respond to the changes, the clock cannot be turned back. Numerous studies have demonstrated that one of the strongest indicators of a child's success in school is the degree of parental involvement in their education. Indeed, we should do everything possible to foster such involvement. But we have to remember that we're asking it of a populace that is less likely to have as much time to devote to its children's schooling than it did in the era of "Leave It To Beaver."

THE ECONOMY

Economists use the word "restructuring." In plain English, that's a big change that affects many people in irreversible ways. The recession of the early 1990s has prompted the biggest restructuring in the Canadian economy since the Depression of the 1930s.

Official unemployment figures—which tell only part of the story—say some 1.4 million people in Canada are out of work. Even that large figure ignores the reality of those who have stopped looking for work and people who have lingered longer in school or returned to the books rather than face a fruitless job hunt. In addition to high unemployment, underemployment has increased. Numbers about the extent of part-time work are rarely reported in the media, but they're massive. In March 1995, 2.3 million people—17.5 percent of all those in the labour force—were defined as part-time workers, employed for less than thirty hours a week.

Young people are the hardest hit in all of this. Statistics Canada reported that there were 500,000 fewer young people with jobs in 1994 than before the recession. In March 1995, the unemployment rate for those aged 15 to 24 was 15.8 percent.

Canada is well into the phase of recovering from the recession. Economic growth in 1994 hit 4.2 percent, but employment has not reached its pre-recession levels and shows no signs of doing so. This is not the space to debate the politics of debt versus jobs—that's another book. From the perspective of education, schools must react to the probability that the children in our schools today will graduate into a leaner, meaner Canada with the prospect of a difficult job search, switching careers several times, light-speed technological change, and a lower standard of living than the baby boomers who teach them.

THE IMPLICATIONS

Here's what all of these changes in the social context imply for education: we can't assume that students come to school with no impediments to learning. Despite Canada's reputation as a generous welfare state, we obviously have not solved the country's social problems. Kids come to school with the baggage of their families' neglect or poverty or substance abuse. Their unique backgrounds aren't checked at the door when they set foot in the classroom.

Regardless of one's political stripe, I think everyone can agree that social factors affect kids' learning. Feeling safe and secure is by itself not enough to ensure that kids will learn, but it's hard to learn much of anything if those needs are not met.

We need to acknowledge this consciously and publicly, then act on it. Discussing the way to do that, again, is another book. I'll restrict my comments to say that cutting welfare and unemployment insurance benefits while not attacking the reasons why people are relying on these benefits is not the way to do it.

I propose that our society needs to do a better job in meeting the social needs of kids, especially at a young age. Even in a society that wants to cut the cost of its social programs, that ounce of prevention should be considered a pound of cure in the future. Meeting children's social needs first means they will be able to take advantage of the education we offer. And people with more education are less likely to be unemployed, on welfare, or involved in crime. This is not a mean-spirited attack on people who need the help of social programs. In fact, it's the opposite—it is an attack on the short-sightedness of a society that doesn't pay enough attention to the social needs of the young as a way of decreasing the likelihood they'll need social programs in the future.

Although our education system places more emphasis on children's academic needs than their social needs, that's not the big problem. The real mistake is that society has divorced children's social needs from their academic needs as if the latter can be met without the former. Although the Royal Commission does not call for schools to be the superhuman solution-finders to all the problems, it acknowledges that the problems must be addressed. "When a child is troubled or underfed, or if a child cannot benefit from schooling because of learning or other disabilities, it is the teacher, the other students and the school who must live with these difficulties. The child, or the child's problem, will not simply disappear if untreated. So it is, therefore, in the interest of educators to deal with such problems." [1] It's also in the best interest of our society.

Meanwhile, social problems persist and continue to arrive at the schoolhouse door. Although using the precious time devoted to education to fix the problems may not be the best idea, the schools must respond to the problems that remain unsolved in the most sensitive way possible. In this case, sensitive doesn't mean soft and emotional, but discriminating and fastidious. School counsellors need to find the right way to get at the root of the problems, then hand the job of solving the problems over to other people and agencies in society. Everyone that comes in contact with students must understand the effects of their social problems and try to compensate for them. That means understanding that as a result of their backgrounds and a host of other factors, each student learns in unique ways and at unique rates. Most important, the school system must act on this understanding.

The job our society has set out for the education system isn't easy. Schools must prepare kids for a future that no one can envisage and for a competitive and, at times, unfriendly economic climate. Schools must produce critical, independent thinkers who have the skills to respond creatively to problems with innovative solutions. Schools must ensure that every student learns a certain amount of the rapidly expanding body of knowledge in the world. And we ask them to do it for the average cost of less than $6,000 per student per year.

THE POLITICAL CLIMATE

The social forces influencing the children in British Columbia's schools in recent years weren't the only factors that had an impact on school reform. If they were, the reforms proposed would probably have proceeded with little fuss and with the public cheering them as the right thing to do. However, meeting the social needs of children was not exactly fashionable in Canada in the early 1990s. The result of the recent jobless economic recovery has not been a public clamour for jobs. Instead, issues of debt and deficit have dominated the political agenda.

Although British Columbia's economy—fuelled by immigration from inside and outside Canada—boomed during the early 1990s, the psychological effects of the global recession weren't held at bay by the Rockies, the U.S. border, and the Pacific Ocean. Here and throughout Canada, the downturn manifested itself politically in fixation with the debt and deficit, which the widely accepted wisdom suddenly portrayed as a crisis. This is not to say it's irrelevant. The point is simply that it prompted a vast shift in public opinion in Canada. Suddenly, talk show babble emphasized cuts to social programs; "BCTV News" fuelled the fires with its daily image of the ticking debt clock erected by the Vancouver Board of Trade; a New York bond-rating agency became a household name. Rather than being seen as a buffer protecting people who fall, the social safety net was depicted as a web entangling the free market. The Reform party rode the conservative wave with its populist sloganeering about "the common sense of the common people."

In this climate, a shift in emphasis toward the social needs of kids could be easily dismissed as hogwash. It's bad timing for left-of-centre education reform.

Lest anyone think British Columbians rejected right-wing assumptions by choosing the leftist New Democrats to run the province, the notion should be dispelled. The New Democrats won for two reasons: the embarrassing, scandal-plagued final few years of the Social Credit government and the sudden rise in credibility of the Liberal party, which had languished on the fringes of B.C. politics long enough to be irrelevant.

It's possible that one of these reasons alone would have been enough to ensure an NDP victory: the Socreds lost virtually all their credibility under Premier Bill Vander Zalm and the New Democrats seemed the only reasonable alternative. So the vote for the NDP was in many ways a vote against Social Credit.

But the NDP win was assured in the blink of an eye during a television debate when hitherto-unknown Liberal leader Gordon Wilson—sharing British Columbians' television screens with the NDP's Mike Harcourt and Socred Premier Rita Johnston—stared at the cameras during a heated exchange between the two and declared that their confrontation demonstrated precisely what was wrong with B.C.'s politics of extremism. The media loved it and so did the public, and suddenly, the Liberals were no longer classed as "other" in the public opinion polls. What the party's newfound credibility provided was an alternative for right-wing voters who were angered by the excesses under Vander Zalm but couldn't put an X beside an NDP candidate's name even while holding their noses. In the end, the two right-of-centre parties captured 57.3 percent of the popular vote, while the NDP managed only 40.7 percent, yet secured a hefty majority of seats.

Although British Columbians ended up with a left-leaning government, the majority of voters wanted a right-wing party in power. And this book will show how the NDP's sensitivity to public opinion made it choose to cancel education reforms that leaned to the left of centre and buy into a more conservative agenda for schools.

Throughout Canada, the rightward shift created a climate of public opinion that fostered criticism of public institutions—not necessarily a bad thing. Government in all its forms was under the microscope not only for waste and inefficiency but for fundamental questions about its role in society. Respect for everyone associated with our public institutions crumbled. It was in some ways a public revolt against experts.

The education system was not immune to the same scrutiny. Like the local paper, lawyers, taxes, and the music that kids listen to, schools joined the list of things people regularly complain about.

"Our schools are failing" became the conventional wisdom, despite evidence to the contrary. In the prevailing political climate, even parents with children in school joined in the chorus, many out of fear that given the economic outlook, their children weren't going to find jobs with the education they were receiving.

One constant in public-opinion polling throughout North America shows that people who don't have children in school are less likely to approve of the performance of the education system than those who do. In general, the less contact one has with a school the lower one's approval rating of the school system will be. Changing demographics mean only a minority of voters have children in school today. And with fewer stay-at-home parents, those who do have children in school don't have as much time to keep in close contact with the institution as the parents of a generation or more ago.

The effect of the political and public-opinion climate on education in Canada is documented in the book *Class Warfare*. Authors Maude Barlow and Heather-jane Robertson attack the arguments that our graduates don't have the skills for the workforce and that business is creating highly skilled jobs. In fact, the evidence shows the opposite is true: Canadians are more highly educated than ever before, and the economic recovery since the recession has not come with increased employment.

The authors show how the climate of fear gave strength to movements that criticized our schools as failing, prompting a demand for so-called back-to-basics education reforms, in stark contrast to the emphasis on social needs and creative thinking suggested by the changing society and changing economy.

All of this set the stage for a divisive debate about education in British Columbia.

THE POLITICS OF EDUCATION IN B.C.

The B.C. Teachers' Federation started to express itself overtly in a political way in 1969 by giving money to the NDP. In the 1972 election campaign, the teachers were instrumental in the victory of Dave Barrett and the New Democrats. The teachers rubbed Social Credit's nose in its defeat, bragging about their role as kingmakers. The Socreds did not forget and reclaimed power in 1975. Says Tom Fleming, a historian and education professor at the University of Victoria, "If you depict the Socreds as used car salesmen, how do you expect to be treated?"

In the boom years of the late 1970s, teachers enjoyed huge wage increases in the 16 to 19 percent range and the rate of hiring out-stripped student enrolment. In the 1980s, government decided to turn back the clock on what it described as the excesses of the preceding years. The province entered the period known as "restraint," setting a nasty political tone for the relationship between government and the education community. Crawford Kilian's 1985 book *School Wars: The Assault on B.C. Education* tells the story most thoroughly, albeit from a decidedly anti-Socred perspective. Tom Fleming adds this editorial comment: "Government was battered and bruised by events of the '80s. Crawford Kilian saw the damage to the system but not to the confidence of the government."

In 1984, Education Minister Jack Heinrich offered an olive branch to teachers as an overture to end the "school wars." He established a provincial school review committee, which in 1985 produced a series of documents called *Let's Talk About Schools*. In many ways, this report is kin to the Royal Commission report. The inquiries took place only two years apart. Many of the key players on the review committee held important positions on the Royal Commission: Tom Fleming wrote *Let's Talk About Schools* and was editor-in-chief of the Royal Commission report; Arthur Kratzmann was information line coordinator for *Let's Talk*, then became Barry Sullivan's deputy commissioner. Todd Rogers was director of research for both reviews.

Meanwhile, fractious teacher-government relations continued. It's essential to understand that the school reform process takes place in the years immediately following the granting of full collective bargaining rights to teachers. Until 1987, the B.C. Teachers' Federation was not a union. It was an association in which membership was required by law for all teachers and principals. In turn, the BCTF established local associations in each district. All teaching staff belonged to these associations, which bargained salaries and some working conditions.

In 1987, the Socreds introduced two controversial pieces of legislation. Bill 19, the Industrial Relations Act, gave full collective bargaining rights to teachers but excluded principals and vice-principals from unionizing. Bill 20, the Teaching Profession Act, established a College of Teachers, ostensibly to govern the professional aspects of teaching. But in doing so, the bill also removed compulsory membership in the BCTF, an attempt to weaken its power.

The combined effect of Bills 19 and 20 made joining the federation merely an option for the local teachers' associations and at the same time presented them with an alternative: the professional College of Teachers' body. Charles Ungerleider, UBC's associate dean of teacher education and an avid watcher of the province's education politics, argues that the Socreds were gambling on the divided loyalties of teachers, forcing them to choose between a trade union and a professional body. "The government believed that the College of Teachers would appear an attractive alternative to teachers faced with pressure to certify as members of local trade unions," writes Ungerleider. He says the Socreds "believed that the College of Teachers would challenge and eventually 'vanquish' the BCTF."[2]

The strategy backfired. All seventy-five district associations chose membership in the BCTF. Although this solidified the federation's power base, as a trade union it was still an infant. It faced criticism from organized labour for not embracing more heartily the ideals of the trade-union movement and for not joining the B.C. Federation of Labour or the Canadian Labour Congress. Meanwhile, it remained wary of what tricks the government would try to pull next. This meant the leadership focused their energy and attention on basic issues of wages, benefits, and the union's survival. Any overtures from the government were greeted with heavy doses of scepticism.

The school wars weren't only between the government and the teachers: trustees have battled the government and the teachers have battled the trustees. Of course, school trustees met face-to-face across the bargaining table with the teachers, a scenario that creates few friendships. But there are further examples of this multidimensional conflict.

For instance, the government passed legislation in 1982 (Education [Interim] Finance Act) capping school district budgets and forcing boards of trustees to submit their own budgets to Victoria for approval. When Vancouver trustees refused to meet the government's budgetary guideline in 1985, Education Minister Jack Heinrich dissolved the board and cabinet appointed a caretaker trustee.

In addition, people who work for the Education Ministry aren't best of friends with those in the field. Teachers and principals can make more money than middle-level bureaucrats, which causes some resentment, and a superintendent's salary can be higher than anybody's in the ministry, including the deputy minister's. The practice of "seconding" (temporarily transferring) teachers and administrators into the ministry for such work as curriculum development (to be paid at their school district rate) pushed the wage discrepancies even more abruptly in the face of the ministry staff, creating further hard feelings.

What this all means is that the events of this book do not take place in an atmosphere of great trust. From the perspective of an outsider, like UBC dean of education Nancy Sheehan, who came to

B.C. from Alberta in 1987, such turmoil in an education system is unprecedented. "I thought I'd crossed over the mountains and gone to loco-land," says Sheehan, adding that she was "horrified by the animosity here." Keep this animosity in mind as the story of education reform unfolds.

THE RESULT

This then is the context: a climate of mistrust among the key players; a union in its infancy; a right-wing government with little credibility in its dying days followed by a left-wing government without a strong mandate for social democratic politics; conservative economic principles triumphing in the court of public opinion; a mood among voters that grows grumpier by the month. These are powerful forces pitched against the social imperatives sketched earlier in this chapter: the changing nature of the family, the ethnic mix, and the economy.

Which wins out? That's the story of this book.

---

1.   Barry Sullivan, *A Legacy for Learners*, p. 71.

2.   Charles Ungerleider, "Power, Politics and the Professionalization of Teachers in British Columbia," p. 374.

[2]
BARRY SULLIVAN'S LEGACY

When he was appointed to lead a Royal Commission with a mandate to examine all aspects of British Columbia's school system, Barry Sullivan admitted he knew little about education. The lawyer's most intense contact with the school system came in 1986 when he was the Crown counsel in the notorious sexual abuse case of Robert Noyes, a principal convicted on nineteen counts of molesting children at schools throughout the province. Sullivan then prepared a general report for the Education and Health Ministries and the Attorney-General on sexual abuse of B.C. schoolchildren by employees.

In retrospect, the critics who slammed Sullivan's appointment in March 1987 look a little strident. Vancouver school board chairman Ken Denike said someone with no background in education would be unfit to head the commission and sent a letter to Premier Bill Vander Zalm protesting the choice of Sullivan. The BCTF, meanwhile, boycotted the very commission it demanded.

The critics saw the Sullivan commission as a quick Socred scam, a Vander Zalm ploy. Perhaps it was. After all, the premier promised the Royal Commission in August 1986 during the previous election campaign. The immediate reaction is best described as derisive laughter. After their attack on schools, why should anyone accept at face value the government's pledge for a thorough and fair look at the education system?

But what the critics didn't count on was the Sullivan factor. The man was committed to the task he took on, committed to hearing the views of the people who came before him, and refused to compromise the integrity of the commission. Sullivan "appealed to public gatherings," says Arthur Kratzmann, the deputy commissioner. "He had a quiet listening dignity no matter where people came from, no matter what their point of view. Some people came out to damn the commission and stayed around to talk to him afterwards." He says Sullivan's message to the commission team was, "If we can't build bridges and get people linking arms, we will have failed."

Over time, respect for Sullivan and the commission grew. The BCTF's policy started with a refusal to play any active role in the commission, while allowing its local associations and provincial specialist associations (the groups representing, for instance, English teachers, school counsellors, etc.) to make up their own minds. Part way through the hearings phase, confronted by tremendous public support and input, more and more of the associations started to participate and finally the BCTF decided to submit a brief.

"We started out with an estimate of maybe a couple of hundred briefs and maybe we could get by with 30 or 40 public meetings," says Kratzmann. In the end: 2,339 oral and written briefs, 66 public hearings. "We could have added many more," says Kratzmann. A Royal Commission is the biggest public consultation mechanism a government has at its disposal. In its thoroughness, the Sullivan commission tapped the mood of the public. Voters could not honestly say they weren't consulted about the education changes that were to come.

Sullivan set about his task by conceiving the six key questions that would form the structure for the final commission report: Who are the people who send students to school? Who are the students? What kind of programs do we need for the students? What kind of people do we need to present the programs? How do we finance the programs? What kind of systems do we use to administer the programs?

These questions framed the mandate for six commissioned papers (on schools and society, students, curriculum, teachers, finance, and governance) which are lesser known among the public, yet which dictated much of what ended up in the commission recommendations. Sullivan hired some of the brightest minds in B.C. education to prepare the research reports. To choose the researchers, the commission asked the various education special-interest groups to nominate the best people for the job. "We got respect that way. People started to realize this is for real," says Kratzmann, adding that the same names were suggested over and over.

The result was that the six research groups were each led by university academics called research directors. Under them was a mix of "senior researchers" made up mostly of superintendents and district administration staff. These teams were given free rein to develop their reports, relying both on the written and verbal submissions to the commission and on reviews of the applicable academic literature. Their research papers were submitted in the spring of 1988—a few months before the final commission report was due—and they shaped the contents of the report.

"We became the commission," says Tom Fleming, research director for the schools and society paper. In fact, although Sullivan's name is on the cover, Fleming (credited as editor) wrote the commission report.

Barely three months into the Royal Commission, Barry Sullivan had a seizure. Arthur Kratzmann hid his illness from the rest of the team until the following Christmas, when Sullivan became too ill to chair commission hearings. It was brain cancer.

"You wouldn't believe the guts this man had and never wimped once, not once," says Kratzmann during an emotional recollection of a man he respected deeply.

If the six research teams became the commission, Kratzmann became the de facto commissioner, although he would never say so himself, as Sullivan was in the hospital more often than he was in his office. Toward the end of the commission's tenure, his ability to speak deteriorated such that he could often answer questions only with yes or no. To some, this might imply that Sullivan had little impact on the contents of the report, but people who served on the commission say that during their think-tank sessions, they always asked aloud the question, "Is this what Barry would want?"

In July 1988, Sullivan could barely grasp the contents of the final report handed to him in the hospital ward, moments before it went to the Queen's Printer. Recalls Kratzmann, "He hadn't spoken a word for weeks and he just looked at it, glanced through and said, 'Fantastic.' " The 265-page report was released to the public August 4, 1988. It contained 83 recommendations: 15 on curriculum, 12 on teaching, 19 on finance, and 37 on governance and administration.

Sullivan had chosen the title of his report as soon as he was appointed commissioner in March 1987. With an almost eerie foresight, he called it *A Legacy for Learners*.

Barry Sullivan died March 21, 1989. He was forty-eight.

CURRICULUM

Since the controversy covered in this book concerns a proposal for massive change to the curriculum, special emphasis on the Royal Commission recommendations in this area is necessary.

Two of the key recommendations in the curriculum section that had a strong impact on the government's immediate actions called for eliminating the grade structure in primary years (kindergarten to grade 3) and for using children's level of development rather than their chronological age to determine when they're ready to enter school.

The commission also envisaged a "common curriculum" from grades 1 through 10 based on four categories of subject matter: humanities, sciences, fine arts, and practical arts (industrial education, business education, physical education, and home economics). Throughout the years of the common curriculum, said the commission, staff should use "an interdisciplinary approach" in their teaching, work in interdisciplinary teams, and teach at least two different subjects. To assist, it said the Education Ministry should develop curriculum documents that provide examples of the interdisciplinary approach and that education faculties should develop courses to prepare teachers in such an approach. The commission also encouraged experimenting with multi-grade classrooms.

Other recommendations for grades 1 to 10 included assigning a "teacher advisor" or "mentor" to each student and limiting the provincially prescribed curriculum to 80 percent of instructional time, leaving 20 percent of the school year for locally developed courses. Finally, in an effort to emphasize choice in the final years of public school, it called for a "certificate of entitlement" to two more years of secondary education for those who complete the common curriculum.

The recommendations covering grades 11 and 12 said graduation requirements should be reviewed with an eye to expanding choice in course selection and grade 12 provincial exams should be assigned in all subjects and count for one-third of the course mark.

A catch-all of further curriculum recommendations emphasized lifelong learning, smaller, more frequent curriculum revisions, funding for extracurricular activities, and narrower goals for the Provincial Learning Assessment Program (designed to assess the knowledge levels of children in the system as a whole).

It's worthwhile to take a closer look at the reasons behind some of the key curriculum recommendations. The interdisciplinary approach (also known as integration of subjects) was an attempt to get away from the university pattern of distinct disciplines that chops the school day up into seemingly unrelated chunks and forces kids in their early teens to deal with as many as eight different teachers after being accustomed to one teacher per year in their first eight years of schooling. In addition, the recommendation for teacher advisors sought to reduce the alienation of kids in the secondary grades. Since students see so many teachers and since teachers instruct so many different students, secondary school provides plenty of room for kids to get lost in the shuffle, neither a healthy nor secure environment for students going through the difficult phase of adolescence.

The techniques that teachers were already using in the primary grades influenced the commission heavily. The recommendations for the primary years also reflected current research showing that developmental factors—not intrinsic intelligence—have the most profound impact on a child's success in school in the early grades. To compensate for the vastly different levels of development among children, the commission envisaged a system that would see each child start school when ready and proceed through the program as he or she learns the appropriate skills. In practice it would mean children would not "fail" in the primary grades, a concept that would later be criticized as a lack of standards. In fact, what it meant was that the arbitrary time lines (a child must learn X by the end of June) were removed. Rather than being chopped into four distinct years with a finish line at the end of each year, the finish line was moved to the end of the four-year program. It reflected the concept of continuous progress (the notion that students shouldn't be forced to repeat an entire subject if they don't reach the finish line by June; rather, they should pick it up from where they left off). The idea that two dozen unique kids in each class would not be required to move in lock-step formation through course material was something that Sullivan and his colleagues liked. They also appreciated primary teachers' emphasis on individualized instruction, integration of subjects, and the benefits of cross-grade classrooms. "We said continue to do as much of that as you can at the intermediate level," says Kratzmann.

TEACHING

Most of the recommendations in this section concerned administrative guidelines for certifying and preparing new teachers, with little impact on the day-to-day working lives of existing teachers. There was also a motherhood statement calling for "a program designed to raise the status of teaching as a career" and three recommendations on professional development: that the BCTF begin professional development programs aimed at improving classroom instruction, that the Education Ministry's funding formula help make regular, extended periods of professional development more readily available, and that "pro-d" programs be improved in rural areas.

FINANCE

Long the bugbear of the B.C. school system, finance drew much attention from the people who spoke to the Royal Commission, from the commission itself, and in turn from the government.

The nineteen recommendations spoke to the collection of property taxes, the ratio of cost-sharing between the province and school districts, the system for approving capital expenditures, and financial accountability.

The most profound financial changes recommended focused on a switch to "block funding," designed to give more stability to the widely fluctuating education budgets designated by the province to the districts. The commission also asked that the province stop using its funding framework as a stick and keep its nose out of school districts' collective bargaining.

What is most remarkable about the commission's recommendations in this area is that they had a calming effect on the school wars. Consequently, finance played little role in the ensuing debate over educational programs that is the focus of this book.

SUPPORT SYSTEMS

The final set of recommendations—thirty-seven in all—covered a wide range of issues that included the length of school trustees' terms, the employment structure of district administration, and special recommendations speaking to the unique situations of rural areas, private schools, home schooling, First Nations students, special-needs children, and female staff and students.

For the purposes of this book, five require special note. The commission called for: 1) an "Education Advisory Council" (EAC) made up of representatives from the BCTF, BCSTA, superintendents, principals, universities, independent schools, parents, students, business, labour, the arts, and the field of science to advise the ministry on policy; 2) as a standing committee of EAC, a Provincial Curriculum Committee to advise the ministry on matters affecting curriculum development, implementation, and evaluation; 3) parent advisory committees in each district and school; 4) services to schoolchildren in need according to mandates developed by the Attorney General and the Social Services, Health, and Education ministries; and 5) a rewrite of the School Act.

RATIONALE FOR THE RECOMMENDATIONS

The Royal Commission report laid bare education as an ideological and political issue, frankly discussing the debate over what we want from our school system in left-right terms. In the end, the report itself was a blend that reflected the demands for both equity and excellence, hard-edged yet nurturing. For the right, it had accountability, for the left, equality, says Tom Fleming. "I tried to make it delicately poised in between and around those concepts." Noting that he has "worked for all the different sets of rascals," Fleming says he tries to steer the ship of state toward the centre, staying away from the rocks on either side, paying equal homage to the motivations of equality on the left and liberty on the right.

Politically, it was a middle-of-the-road document, but with a slight lean toward the left lane, if for no other reason than the fact that education in North America has generally been conservative and the reality that the party in power in B.C. for all but three years in the previous four decades had been the right-wing Social Credit. To get to the centre required a shift in direction to the left. "If you want to put colours on it [the report], it's more red than blue," says Arthur Kratzmann.

Tarry Grieve, now superintendent of the Kamloops district and co-author of the research paper on students, conceives of the Royal Commission as a pragmatic compromise between the competing philosophies that tug at education. "The Royal Commission was not promoting bandwagons. It says we must have the ability to adapt and be flexible."

This philosophy of adaptability is best expressed in the last chapter of the Royal Commission report, which discusses the problem of developing a mandate for a school system faced with the tension that is the result of competing ideologies. The resulting portrait that the commission draws is of a system that should be both "loose and tight." Loose means greater diversity and freedom for the staff and students in the system. Tight means recommendations that funding be more predictable, accountability be strengthened, responsibilities be more clearly defined, and communication be enhanced.

Fleming discussed this concept further in an address to the BCSTA on January 26, 1989, the day before the government announced its response to the commission. He described the demanding intellectual exercise of reconciling the conflicting points of view presented to the commission by the public: the call for excellence and equity, parental involvement and professional autonomy, choice and standardization, diversity and accountability, and other themes like predictability, access, and relevance. To achieve its goal, the commission needed an all-encompassing view of the system that struck a balance between the age-old competing forces: the best interests of the individual versus the best interests of society. Rather than choose one or the other, the team looked for a philosophy that could meet both and reduce uncertainty without reducing flexibility. Hence the mix of recommendations that emphasized loosening or tightening different parts of the system.

Once the commission's framework becomes clear, it can be readily seen why they made the recommendations they did: on the one hand, free up time for local courses, encourage home schooling, reduce restrictions on graduation requirements, and make primary ungraded; on the other hand, invoke block funding, make teachers teach two subjects, expand provincial exams, mandate involvement of parents and the lobby groups, and increase coordination of social services through schools.

In many ways, it was a document that whittled away at the foundations of the old power relationships. It called for a certain transfer of power from the hands of those higher in the education chain toward those lower. The less power people had in the past, the more it gave them, and vice versa. It empowered students, parents, and teachers, while reducing the power of the Education Ministry and, to a lesser extent, district administration. The commission was arguing, "The best use of limited resources is maximum power at the job site," says Tarry Grieve. This was the most revolutionary aspect of the Royal Commission.

"We weren't all that revolutionary in our recommendations," says Arthur Kratzmann. "We just changed the structure a little." But it's that change in structure that was so profound. It invoked the theme of partnership, of decentralization of decision-making away from the ministry, and a tone that would move the province away from the fractiousness of the preceding years.

The reaction was almost unanimous support. Although critics took issue with certain recommendations—the entitlement certificate after grade 10 being the most frequent target—the thrust of the report was greeted warmly even by the government's opponents. "It seemed to open up a really broad debate about the system in a very positive way," says Ken Novakowski, then the BCTF vice-president. He says the report "was basically supportive" of education in B.C. yet also revealed "a lot of possibilities for a strong and better education system."

Jackie Tegart, former BCSTA president, calls it "an excellent report that reflected the community and the people that made presentations. I really believe the Royal Commission took lots of risks in their recommendations."

"People really did want peace in our time," says Tom Fleming. "We were operating in a volatile time. What surprised me was how much faith the province had in us."

Basically, the timing was ripe to declare a truce in the school wars. Suddenly, *A Legacy for Learners* offered a face-saving treaty for all sides. In Fleming's words, it became "radioactive—people couldn't stay away from it."

"People were ready and this created a catalyst for folks to get together and talk about education," says Kratzmann. "If you saw what was happening a month before the commission started and a month after the commission report was out, you just almost see two worlds. [Before the commission] we had teachers who wouldn't talk to the government unless it was absolutely critical. We had the executive director of the trustees association and the executive director of the BCTF meeting quietly over lunch because they couldn't get their executives to meet together. All sorts of crazy things going on, people shaking fists at each other."

In the months that followed, instead of shaking fists, people started shaking hands, albeit stiffly. Says Kratzmann, "We got on with the business of at least discussing education and having some people working at doing some new things. Whether they were the right ones or not, it was a big gain. I was sitting back and smiling and saying, 'Barry, I hope you can see this.'"

The impact of Sullivan's death on the events to follow is an important factor, yet little discussed in the public realm. Kratzmann, as assistant commissioner, seemed the obvious second choice to champion the commission. He was front and centre for the report's release, but only because someone had to be. He faded into the background immediately thereafter, tramping around his Australian homeland and elsewhere for two years. This was not accidental. As Kratzmann sees it, had he stayed around the province, he would indeed have been the person contacted by the media and the ministry to speak for the commission as it worked its way through the resulting process. "First thing you know, the edge of Sullivan would have come off this and I felt maybe some of the Kratzmann insignia would go on it," he says. "The fellow had so much courage that I said to myself, 'This is going to stay solidly as the Sullivan commission.'"

The rest of the commission's staff were employees who submitted their research reports, then went back to their regular jobs. The staff knew there would be demands to speak about the commission, but says Robin Brayne, who co-wrote the report on teachers, "We decided none of us had the power nor had the mandate nor had the authority."

Consequently, there was no "advocate" for the commission.

"We have not had a champion for the Royal Commission since Barry Sullivan's death and that is a real shame," says Jackie Tegart of the BCSTA.

"If Sullivan had been healthy, maybe he would have been able to afford to continue to devote part of his attention to what happened with this child of his," says David Robitaille, the UBC professor who served as research director for the curriculum paper.

We can only speculate what would have changed had Barry Sullivan lived. Sullivan wasn't around to keep an eye on the process that followed the release of his report and the perception that his intentions were betrayed is out there. Many people involved in the Royal Commission see the government's translation of the report into policy as an aberration of the commission's recommendations. It's a point that's addressed in the next chapter.

Barry Sullivan's legacy was a document that has profoundly influenced the debate about education in B.C. for the last seven years and appears poised to continue its influence well into the next decade. People in the school system regularly speak of the report as a kind of guiding light. Perhaps this romanticizes the document and overlooks its flaws. However, *A Legacy for Learners* did offer the laudable vision of a system that treats its students more as unique individuals than as a large pool of kids who fit into predetermined slots. The document's most important immediate effect was, if not an end to the school wars over finance, certainly a cease-fire.

But the battle over curriculum was about to begin.

[3]
YEAR 2000

There's a story that an education professor from England visited British Columbia, examined Year 2000, and said, "This must have been a very left-wing government that came up with this program," adding that the Labour Party in the U.K. would be afraid of promoting such a plan.

The irony is that Year 2000 was introduced by the decidedly conservative government of Social Credit. What prompted the Vander Zalm government to plough ahead with what some opponents would ultimately label a left-wing school program?

Several theories make the rounds. "The Royal Commission report recommendations seemed to be reasonable and presented an opportunity for government to develop a refreshed blueprint for the education system," says a high-level bureaucrat. "Government saw it as covering a number of important bases to develop a better sense of cohesion and direction in the system."

"For a centre-right group of politicians to accept what is really a revolutionary change in approach to education . . . I thought we would have a lot more difficulty than we had with the cabinet," says Sandy Peel, the deputy minister of the day. He says cabinet members agreed because groups they respected—like the B.C. Business Council and the chambers of commerce—wanted this kind of change to the education system.

But Peel also gives credit to the man that most people point to as the driving force behind Year 2000: Education Minister Tony Brummet.

Tony Brummet is a crusty, straight-talking former school principal who spent much of his career in the hard-working northern town of Fort St. John, and he's considered by some to be the best education minister this province has ever seen.

"Tony Brummet was a very good minister of education," says Burnaby superintendent Elmer Froese. "His educational assumptions came from the time when he was a very popular and effective principal of a junior secondary school in northern British Columbia. Highly populist, very respectful of teachers and students, very responsive, well-liked as an educator. Tony Brummet resonated with the values of what he as a young principal in the 1960s believed was good for kids. Now, when he was Minister of Education, those same principles came from the Royal Commission. He agreed with them intuitively, professionally."

Another reason why Brummet championed the Royal Commission recommendations was the bond he formed with Barry Sullivan. The two men "would meet and talk about everything under the sun, except the commission," says one insider. "They talked about trucking and sports and mining and little by little I saw a tremendous bond forming." Brummet used to visit Sullivan in the cancer clinic, entering through a back door. Sometimes he held the dying man's hand. "Tony Brummet assured Barry Sullivan's family that this commission wouldn't gather dust on the shelves," says the source.

Brummet denies this, however. He says only that he "developed a high regard for Barry Sullivan" during the process and says it wouldn't have been appropriate for the education minister to meet with the commissioner.

There's a belief among some in education that Brummet single-handedly persuaded cabinet to adopt the recommendations of the Royal Commission. How did he do it? "I can only guess that Mr. Brummet was a very good salesman," says Len Fox, the Socred MLA-turned-Reform education critic.

Some say he sold them on accepting the policies because they would bring greater accountability into the system. Others say he persuaded the Socreds that the plan would defuse education as an election issue next time round by stealing the NDP's ammunition. Still others say he pulled the wool over cabinet's eyes. "Do you really think the Socreds knew what they were doing?" asks Marv Wideen, SFU education professor, adding that Year 2000 crept into government as a Trojan horse.

There's no question Brummet had clout in caucus and cabinet. His head had been on the Vander Zalm chopping block at the time of the Royal Commission hearings. He was called to an evening meeting in the premier's office at which certain cabinet ministers were going to get the boot. But before Vander Zalm acted, he faced a revolt from longtime Socreds, including Grace McCarthy, who told him he'd gone too far. Brummet survived the would-be purge and as one observer tells me, "I could visibly see from that day on Tony could flutter his wings a little more and felt a little stronger in office."

"Tony believed in what the Sullivan report said. He believed in the focus on the individual. He believed very strongly that critical thinking and problem-solving needed to be focused on in schools," says Sandy Peel. He says Brummet persuaded cabinet that education mattered and was a significant investment.

But what Peel doesn't mention is his own role in the story. Brummet and Peel were a kind of dynamic duo of education. Even a traditional ministry opponent like the BCTF's Ken Novakowski couldn't help but praise the pair. "With the combination of Peel and the minister, education benefited," he said. "Peel was able to exercise more influence on the inside circle than any other previous deputy minister."[1]

Peel, who came to the position in 1987, was the first deputy minister of education not to hold a teaching certificate. His background was in transportation, as a former head of Transport Canada's eastern rail and ferry operations. He came to the position knowing his way around money and understanding industry. Peel was particularly impressed by the Japanese model in which companies function on consensus. In applying this to the pending education change, he decided, "If there isn't consensus, it's not going to work."

"It's hard to imagine a system that is more difficult to manage than the education system," Peel continues, "because you've got a ministry that is responsible for the overall policy, the curriculum, the funding formulas, and all that, you've got school districts that do all the negotiating, and then finally you've got a teacher that walks into the classroom, closes the door and it's all up to the teacher. What happens in the classroom is 100 percent the teacher, so if the system is going to work, you've got to have people buy into it. The teachers have to buy into it, trustees have to buy into it, parents have to buy into it, the business community has to buy into it. That was the reason for the advisory council [EAC]—these are the people to whom education counts."

Brummet tells a similar official version, concentrating on the educational benefits of the proposals. "I thought it was an educational move, not a political move," says Brummet. The focus on the learner, individualized instruction, flexibility, and getting kids excited about learning were better than "making them go through hoops," he says.

The romantic notion of Brummet as champion of education holds sway over most. In fact, the reason the government was willing to adopt the Royal Commission had less to do with Brummet's salesmanship and charisma and more to do with persuading the public that Social Credit cared about education.

"The Socreds had pushed the limits of education bashing," says Charles Ungerleider of UBC. Government polling had revealed that the public was fed up with cuts in education. More importantly, the Socreds found out they could garner as much interest and acclaim—and as many votes—by being positive about education as they would from being negative.

This is backed up by the results of a July 1988 strategic communications study labelled "for internal purposes only." This report reveals that the face the government put on education after the Royal Commission was as much strategy as substance. The study was conducted in the summer of 1988 by Decima Research and I obtained a copy through a Freedom of Information request. In it, the pollsters say the government faced "The Big Choice": continue the past, characterized in the public's mind by conflict, cuts, and an anti-teacher approach; or take a new course characterized by a strong commitment to consultation, partnership, adequate finances, and quality education for students, reassuring the public that the basics are being taught and creative opportunities are available. "The public's expectation of 'continuation of the old way' is so deeply rooted that a shift to the second choice can only be accomplished through a dramatic, sustained and believable change,"[2] said the report. It suggested the government choose option number two and added the following recommendations: Premier Vander Zalm "should remain silent on education matters pending Cabinet's consideration of the Brummet proposals due December 1, 1988. . . . The role of the Premier in the education portfolio (BCTF-bashing, rejecting hungry kids, privatization letters to teachers, etc.) is seen almost unanimously as a barrier to the re-establishment of confidence in the public education system."[3] The plan also called for Brummet to become "Mr. Education" in B.C. "As a former principal, he is well-positioned. He has good credibility with system stakeholders. . . . Whenever possible, he should be seen speaking with and listening to local principals, teachers, parents, superintendents and trustees."[4] Decima also said Sandy Peel should do the same.

The first step in turning around the public attitude would be to milk the Royal Commission. The report said, "The Royal Commission report should be 'ridden' for all its worth by the Minister and the Ministry."[5] It recommended more effort on good media relations and a cross-province consultation tour by the minister.

So the powerful pair of Peel and Brummet set about trying to capitalize on the Royal Commission as the chance to change the climate in the province's education system. "We were coming out of years of restraint at that period, the mood between the ministry and the BCSTA and the BCTF was not good," says Peel. "One thing I didn't want to have happen was a Royal Commission report come into government . . . and the government sort of go through all of its policy response before it releases the report." So in an unusual move, cabinet released the report almost immediately after receiving it and started the debate in public.

After the commission recommendations were released, Brummet spent the fall of 1988 travelling around the province to talk about the Sullivan report and solicit reaction, as suggested by the communications strategy. In his words, he was validating that what the commission recommended was an accurate reflection of the will of the province.

"He felt very, very comfortable out and around British Columbia in the various school districts, sitting in the staff rooms, having meetings with parents, and doing those kinds of things," says Peel.

At the same time, the ministry created what it called the Provincial Education Policy Advisory Committee made up of the major education lobbies to discuss the Sullivan report. This group—together with ministry staff under policy and planning director Jerry Mussio—analysed some of the key issues. The purpose was to persuade the stakeholder groups that government policy would be consistent with the Royal Commission. Ultimately, the committee gave cabinet a written response to the Sullivan report that went to cabinet, and cabinet accepted about 95 percent of what the advisory body said. It was the first step toward greater consultation. "We had now started to develop a real cohesiveness amongst the various people because it was a very open process and one that was clearly working," says Peel.

Releasing a document called *Policy Directions*, Brummet announced the government's response to the Royal Commission on January 27, 1989, during a BCSTA conference. A ministry news release trumpeted that the changes resulting from *Policy Directions* would "place greater emphasis on problem-solving and creative thinking as well as reaffirm the importance of ensuring that all students acquire basic literacy skills."[6] To top it off, the government announced $1.4 billion for implementing the policies over the following ten years.

The document stated twenty-three government policies. Some were motherhood statements like, "The multicultural nature of British Columbia society will be recognized through education policy and programs," and "The teaching profession is recognized as being fundamental to the operation of a quality school system." Some were simple changes to existing policy, such as increased funding for some independent schools and recognition of home schooling. The policies also included a mandate for the school system, a permanent Education Advisory Council, and a promise of a new School Act. Finally, at the heart of the document were four key policies marking a new structure for the curriculum from kindergarten to grade 12: two entry points (in September and January) for children starting school; a four-year primary program that wiped out the division between grades; a common curriculum from grade 4 to grade 10 with more integration between subjects; and in the final two years of school, a choice of multiple "pathways" that reflect the career aspirations of a wider range of students.

Officially, the government endorsed all but two of the Royal Commission's eighty-three recommendations—the ones calling for four-year terms of office for trustees and the controversial "entitlement certificate" after grade 10, criticized as an incentive for kids to drop out of school. However, on closer examination, *Policy Directions* is not such a sweeping endorsement of the Sullivan report. According to a BCTF paper from October 1989, the government completely ignored nine Royal Commission recommendations, misinterpreted three others, and undervalued five more.

The federation said the government was silent on the Royal Commission recommendations for: a teacher advisor or mentor; funding for extracurricular activities; recognition for teaching staff who work with student-teachers; special services for first-year teachers; regular extended periods of time off for professional development as well as BCTF involvement in in-service education; better professional development in rural areas; a special program to respond to the deteriorating conditions in schools built immediately after 1945; a standing committee of the Education Advisory Council to give input on curriculum; and additional support services for special-needs students and their teachers.

The BCTF paper also said that by bringing in dual entry, the government misinterpreted the recommendation on using developmental criteria for placing children in the first year of school. It said that by implementing ungraded primary across the province, the government misinterpreted the recommendation for an experiment with multi-graded classrooms. And the paper said the government was moving too quickly with widespread curriculum reform, in defiance of the Royal Commission recommendation that curriculum changes be smaller and more frequent.

Finally, the paper said the government was not providing enough funding for four recommendations about education for First Nations children and was not continuing with a project to eliminate gender stereotypes from curriculum materials.

Despite the differences between the Royal Commission recommendations and the government's policy response, the Education Ministry embarked on a flurry of activity after *Policy Directions* was released. Its three major tasks for the first half of 1989 were to rewrite the School Act based on the policies spelled out in *Policy Directions*, issue a version of the primary program, and write a draft framework document laying the foundation for the entire education program, the document that would become known as Year 2000.

School Act

"I was accused by some parties of having the draft legislation in my drawer the whole time," says Sandy Peel. But in fact the education policy advisory committee was in on every stage of the drafting process until the legislation went in camera to cabinet. "It was very open, very transparent, there was nothing held back, there were no surprises," says Peel.

The government tabled Bill 67, the new School Act on June 26. It legislated two important consultation bodies: the Education Advisory Council, made up of every group with a stake in education, which then-assistant deputy minister Jack Fleming calls "a pretty strong act on the part of government to say we're going to give up on the wars," and parent advisory councils, allowing parents to form groups in each school and district that could advise principals and boards on issues and concerns. The act also recognized home schooling, required districts to produce annual reports, and guaranteed rights for minority linguistic groups, access to personal school records, and appeals of school decisions. It passed without opposition from the NDP.

Along with the new School Act, the Independent School Act (Bill 68) dictated that private schools must receive some public money if they meet provincial standards. It required all private schools to register with the government, but increased the maximum funding available to private schools to 50 percent of the public school per-pupil cost (up from 36 percent).

PRIMARY PROGRAM

On March 1, a group of brightly dressed women marched enthusiastically into the dreary concrete Education Ministry building on Superior Street in Victoria. They were the members of the primary program team and they were about to take the grey-suited ministry by storm.

The primary teachers specialist association of the BCTF had completed a lot of research and program design and had lobbied government for a long time to make formal changes to the primary curriculum. For years, primary teacher education programs had talked about taking a developmental approach to learning. Most primary teachers were using such techniques in their classes already because they represented sound professional practice. These were the ideas that the primary teachers presented in their brief to the Sullivan commission; in turn, these ideas formed the basis for the commission's recommendations and the government's policy. And since teachers made up the team that was charged with translating policy into a program, the primary program had near unanimous support amongst the staff in the field.

"We chose the primary program as the initial thrust on this for one very simple reason: most of the primary teachers teach that way," says Peel. "We don't start to get into the rote lesson plan things until you get into the middle schools and the high schools. We felt if we had that sort of success story get off in that area, it was going to then facilitate leading the others."

YEAR 2000: A FRAMEWORK FOR LEARNING

Much maligned yet much misunderstood, Year 2000 became many different things to many people. It was the reason the schools were producing illiterate graduates. It was a government policy that banned, among other things, sports competitions. It was a sinister attempt to invoke psychotherapeutic techniques on children and promote pagan spirituality.

Year 2000 was none of these, yet it was accused of all of them. In fact, the question "What is Year 2000?" was answered incorrectly more often than "What is the capital of Romania?" on a grade 7 geography test.

Year 2000 was a series of documents spelling out a philosophical framework for education programs in B.C. schools and policy proposals for putting that framework into practice. The term Year 2000 first appeared in September 1989 with a draft document called *Year 2000: A Curriculum and Assessment Framework for the Future.* In 1990, after receiving feedback on the draft, the Education Ministry produced *Year 2000: A Framework for Learning,* a twenty-nine-page document outlining "the foundation for all program development, student assessment and evaluation, and reporting activities in British Columbia." This more than any other document was "the Year 2000." As a framework document, it did not spell out the details of implementation, describe programs, or mandate particular teaching styles. Rather, it was a philosophical tract that laid out principles to be followed. Over the next three years came the documents detailing the proposed design of the education program, divided into three distinct phases: primary (kindergarten to grade 3), intermediate (grades 4 through 10), and graduation (grades 11 and 12). It's important to understand that these three programs were distinct: although they were based on the same principles, the translations were different. Criticism of "Year 2000" as a whole is not constructive: first there was Year 2000 philosophy, then came three different programs, whose merits and flaws must be examined individually. Teams of educators produced various drafts of each document, a process that will be described next chapter. In this chapter, the philosophy at the root of Year 2000 is the focus.

YEAR 2000 PHILOSOPHY

"The kind of teachers whose classrooms parents die to have their children in, the ones they sign up for are the kinds of teachers we were writing about in the Year 2000," says primary teacher Marlene Dergousoff. "The ones they don't want their kids to have are the ones who weren't even paying any attention to those programs."

Year 2000 was often labelled progressive. Not only was this used in a pejorative sense, it was also inaccurate. A precise definition of progressive education is difficult—it means different things to different people. In academic circles, the term refers to the North American progressive education movement of the 1920s, led by John Dewey. Its proponents said children should be treated with dignity and respect—a simple enough principle, but in the 1960s, it manifested itself in such pedagogical disasters as the free schools movement, which made attendance optional, the open-concept classroom, which often descended into disorganized chaos, and social promotion, the idea that students should pass into the next grade even if they haven't learned the required course material, in an effort to prevent stigmatizing them as failures. These screw-ups are what the general public recalls when it hears an education program described as progressive. They are not what Year 2000 called for, so given this understanding of the term, it's not helpful to describe Year 2000 as progressive.

More accurately, Year 2000 philosophy should be described as constructivist but also featuring elements of Piagetian (developmental), Deweyan (active learning), and the child-centred perspectives. Not as catchy as progressive, but this unwieldy label lays the groundwork for more informed debate.

Dewey is considered the father of progressive education, but it's helpful to remember that he was writing at the turn of the century and the progressive movement of the 1960s was not his vision. Dewey focused on the importance of problem-solving and firsthand experience in learning, what is now called active learning. Dewey used the word progressive in reference not to the political meaning of the word (as left-of-centre) but in terms of the progress of learning: students should build gradually on things already learned, first acquiring skills and knowledge that can then be used to gain insights into more complex items. There's no question that Year 2000 borrowed from Dewey even though he is not mentioned in the documents.

"Child-centred" is one of the terms the progressive educators of the 1960s used to describe their conception of schooling. In its pure form, child-centred theory—like Dewey—is critical of the "traditional" method of instruction in which teachers lecture and students absorb (also known as direct instruction or sometimes teacher-centred learning). To child-centred theorists, direct instruction makes the student the passive recipient of information doled out by a teacher. To put the child at the centre requires more active learning, in which the teacher aids and encourages students to find out things for themselves. A couple of metaphors are illustrative. French philosopher Jean-Paul Sartre uses what he calls the "digestive" metaphor to describe the traditional method of teaching: a teacher "feeds" the children with information to "fill them up." The Brazilian educator Paulo Freire describes direct-instruction as "banking"—the teacher "deposits" information into students, who passively, like bank clerks, receive and file the information. Freire says the banking style of teaching stultifies growth and minimizes independent thought, creativity, and problem-solving skills. The opposite—Freire's equivalent to child-centred learning—is what he calls "problem-posing" education. It changes the teacher-student power relationship so that the student and teacher engage in a dialogue. The power relationship is not completely overturned—the teacher still has the important role of aiding and encouraging learning but he or she does so by posing problems that relate to the student's world. In doing so, the teacher enlarges the student's consciousness.

Constructivism is based on the notion that people "construct" understanding by building on what they already know. People learn by comparing new ideas to their previous understandings and trying to make sense of the new information. In other words, they connect new information to previous knowledge and, as a result, construct meaning. "Learning is creating, it is not receiving," write Ronald Marx and Tarry Grieve. "Teaching methods must help learners create knowledge and understanding. This cannot be done effectively by treating learners as passive vessels to be filled with knowledge, but it can be done effectively by requiring learners to work hard and think deeply about the topics to be learned." [7]

Jean Piaget is a Swiss psychologist renowned for his work on the developmental stages of children's thinking. He argues that all children pass through certain stages in their ability to represent items in thought and language and their ability to think about concrete and abstract items, but the rate at which children pass through the stages varies widely. Piaget's research shows that maturity, physical experience, and social interaction are related to children's intellectual development and the rate at which they pass through the stages of thought.

These perspectives are the philosophical precursors of Year 2000. It's time to take a look at what the document Year 2000: A Framework for Learning proposed.

PRINCIPLES OF LEARNING

The most important part of Year 2000 was the section that spelled out three principles of learning. Based on the characteristics of learning discussed in the Royal Commission research paper by Ronald Marx and Tarry Grieve, [8] the three principles were as follows. 1) Learning requires the active participation of the learner. 2) People learn in a variety of ways and at different rates. 3) Learning is both an individual and social process.

ACTIVE PARTICIPATION   Year 2000 said learning is a natural and enjoyable process, but it requires effort. It said people learn by connecting new information to previous knowledge: they place each new idea in the context of what they already know and in doing so construct meaning out of the new idea. To succeed, people need to reflect on what they've learned and need positive feedback when they demonstrate what they've learned.

DIFFERENT RATES AND WAYS OF LEARNING   Despite generalizations that can be made about the methods students use to learn and the speed at which they learn at different ages, there are important differences in each individual's rate and way of learning. How a person learns is not just a function of age but personal interests, abilities and methods, past experience, and the current environment.

INDIVIDUAL AND SOCIAL PROCESS   Students sometimes learn best individually and sometimes they need to discuss their understanding of an idea with others, and the social interaction that occurs builds interpersonal skills.

From these three simple—and difficult to disagree with—principles would stem an entire education program. The implications for teaching were profound. By stating that learning requires the active participation of a student, it meant that teachers should not treat kids as empty vessels to be filled with knowledge by pouring facts in. By stating that students learn in different ways and at different rates, it meant that teachers should not expect all children in a class to proceed through course material at the rate set by the teacher and that teachers must use a variety of instructional techniques. By stating that learning is also a social process, it meant more collaborative and group work.

This called for no less than a revolution in the classroom. From the days of the one-room schoolhouse until the present, traditional teaching methods dominated education. Lectures, drills, repeat-after-me, take notes from the board, watch this video, read chapter six and answer the ten questions at the back of the book: they are the time-honoured techniques of school, each one controlled by the teacher, each one requiring passive receipt of information by the student, each one demanding that all students approach the material in the same way and absorb it in the same period of time. Year 2000's principles of learning were revolutionary because they took some power from teachers and gave it to students.

"The old model of teacher in charge and at centre has got to be destroyed," says Tarry Grieve. "We need a system that is responsive. We have to move away from a system that treats everyone the same. There are different types of learning styles and different types of intelligence." Teachers need to be able to differentiate between children. For instance, says Grieve, critical feedback can be destructive to children with poor self-esteem, especially those from lower-income backgrounds. Such kids are afraid to take risks, so it's wrong for a teacher to put them in a position to make mistakes. But those who are more settled and self-assured need criticism and need to take risks. For them, jumping on a self-esteem bandwagon is no good.

Year 2000 was not telling teachers to throw away the book. It called for a shift in emphasis along the traditional-progressive spectrum. More importantly it called for using certain techniques in certain situations, pointing out that both the traditional and child-centred approaches have merit, if used properly. It said be more sensitive to the differences among kids, don't treat them as if they're all the same.

"It would be foolish to recommend one particular method of teaching as superior to others," wrote Marx and Grieve. "It is quite clear from research that many different teaching methods can be appropriate, depending on many factors, including the subject matter that is being taught, the age of the learners, the background characteristics of the learners, the type of school, and the expertise of the teacher." [9]

Here is how one teacher uses the principles of learning in his classes. Rick Turner teaches English at Brocklehurst Secondary School in Kamloops, now that he has finished his term as president of the district teachers' association. One result of his teaching technique is noisy classes. "I'm getting old and it's hard on my nerves because I don't like that racket, but there's no other way they'll learn," says Turner. He simplifies teaching into two models: telling kids what the teacher knows versus realizing that kids have diverse interests. He believes in the need for a common curriculum so that kids end up literate, numerate, educated in every sense of the word, but there should not be a common body of facts kids must memorize and spit out. Rather than dictate that all the class read a particular story from a book of CanLit, Turner lets the kids pick their own. "I make them more responsible for choosing what they'll study and how they'll demonstrate their knowledge." The object is that they learn the unique properties of Canadian literature in terms of setting, themes, and characters, recognize what makes good writing good, and make a coherent presentation to class.

That's the classroom vision that Sandy Peel, former deputy minister of education, has in mind when he says the whole theme behind the Year 2000 framework was to create critical-thinking, problem-solving students, people who know how to access and use knowledge as opposed to learning it by rote.

PRINCIPLES OF CURRICULUM AND ASSESSMENT

The stated principles of learning implied the need for changes to curriculum and assessment. *Year 2000: A Framework for Learning* said: 1) Curriculum and assessment should be learner-focused; 2) Assessment and reporting should help students make informed choices.

LEARNER-FOCUSED   These two words would cause Year 2000 proponents no end of controversy because they were interpreted to mean the same as "child-centred," one of the buzz-phrases of progressive education. However, the Year 2000 document defined learner-focused in the following ways.

It said curriculum and assessment should be developmentally appropriate: curriculum should reflect the age-related move from concrete toward abstract thought and assessment should relate what students can do in relation to expectations for their age group. That meant taking into account the fact that developmental age and family background—not ability—are the two biggest factors in a child's success in the early years of school. The message was: help kids acquire a solid, secure foundation in school in the early years before exposing them to failure.

It said students should have the chance to be self-directed in their learning: giving them choices within programs, while at the same time ensuring they understand the intent of the exercise. Self-directed learning also encourages kids to evaluate their own performance, to take on challenges, and to pursue excellence.

It said programs and teaching methods should be personalized as much as possible to meet all students' individual needs, to reflect their interests and preferences, and to match their rate of learning. It also said programs and assessment must be relevant and meaningful to students.

The most controversial part of the learner-focused principles said curriculum should allow for continuous progress. As discussed in Chapter 2 in the section on the curriculum recommendations of the Royal Commission, continuous progress means removing arbitrary restrictions that say a student must learn a topic in a specified period of time. It says students can work on subject matter at rates that reflect their individual differences yet challenges them. Students who have trouble will need extra help, alternative teaching approaches, or different resources, but they can eventually learn the material. Here's what else the Year 2000 document added: "With a continuous learning approach, a child is not 'failed' or required to repeat a unit of work because his or her learning rate does not match the expectation for that age group." This sentence was interpreted by many to represent the notion of social promotion: pass a student even if he or she hasn't met the standard. However, that's not what the sentence said. The implication of continuous progress is that some students *need more time* than others to learn certain topics. Let's say I can't learn grade 6 math as quickly as my peers and by June I've only reached as far as fractions. Rather than "fail" the course and be forced to start all over again in September (with five or six months worth of stuff that I already know), under continuous progress, I would be able to pick up where I left off by starting with the unit after fractions.

ASSESSMENT AND REPORTING FOR INFORMED CHOICES   Year 2000 recommended that teachers use a wide range of assessment methods, including a significant amount of self-assessment, to get the best possible picture of a student's achievement. It said students demonstrate their learning in different ways and that competence can be assessed based on more than just tests—writing assignments, oral presentations, pictures, to name a few. Report cards should say what each student can do with reference to what is expected of children at that stage. It added that rarely if ever should a teacher compare the performance of students to others in the class. Instead, teachers should base any relative comparisons of learning on larger groups of students across the district or province.

The other aspects of the Year 2000 framework document included three previously released elements of government policy: a mission statement for the school system, a description of what makes for an educated citizen, and the overall goals of the system. Finally, the framework document sketched the structure of the three provincial programs—primary, intermediate, and graduation.

The mission statement said, "The purpose of the British Columbia school system is to enable learners to develop their individual potential and to acquire the knowledge, skills and attitudes needed to contribute to a healthy society and a prosperous and sustainable economy."

In turn, the government said a healthy society and prosperous and sustainable economy can be achieved by developing "educated citizens"—people who can think critically, communicate from a broad knowledge base, make independent decisions, exercise their democratic rights and responsibilities, and are thoughtful, creative, flexible, self-motivated, skilled, productive, co-operative, and respectful of others.

And in turn, to develop these characteristics in its citizens, the government said the school system must meet certain goals: its prime goal is intellectual development, while the goals it shares with the family and the community are career and social development.

Finally, Year 2000 described in two- to four-page summaries the general features of the primary, intermediate, and graduation programs, indicating that future "foundation" documents would give more explicit detail. Few specific elements were dictated: in the main, the document said teachers would use a variety of instructional techniques, assessment methods, reporting methods, and learning resources (books, videos, etc.) Three important distinctions that were made affected the primary program. Year 2000 said the primary program would be a single entity rather than a series of separate years, so it would not be organized by grades but most students would complete it in four years. Since there were no grades, students would not "fail" at the end of a year. In addition, it said the use of letter grades was not appropriate in the primary years. Third, it said the traditional subjects within the four strands (humanities, sciences, fine arts, and practical arts) were to be integrated.

It's important to note that Year 2000 neither required nor forbade integration and letter grades in the intermediate program: it gave the choice to teachers and schools. It added that continuous progress was important for the intermediate grades and that students should not be forced to repeat a year, as discussed above.

The two-year graduation program was addressed in a little more detail by listing graduation requirements, available options, units of study, provincial examination rules, and the role of student planning for the program with an eye to a future career. Letter grades were mandatory.

"That Year 2000 document A Framework for Learning was really a first attempt to pull together the mission statement, the educated citizen statement, the learning principles (out of the Marx and Grieve report), the primary program design and things that it argued for . . . and envisage a whole system that would be based around that set of constructs," says Jack Fleming, former assistant deputy minister for education programs.

The framework document was designed as the philosophical foundation to be used by the people recruited to the Education Ministry to write the primary, intermediate, and graduation program documents. It's an important process that is addressed in detail in the next three chapters because it is at the heart of what happened. But first, some critical analysis of the philosophies underlying Year 2000 is necessary.

ANALYSIS OF YEAR 2000 PHILOSOPHY

Sources interviewed for this book were able to point out many good things about Year 2000. Many of the problems they pointed out with the philosophy had to do with how it was *interpreted*, not with the philosophy itself.

Year 2000 was praised for trying to meet the needs of students who aren't bound for university; for describing assessment as a way to help students see what they've learned rather than a way to label students as passes or failures; and for its emphasis on making learning more enjoyable and less of a drudgery.

The two most cogent criticisms of Year 2000 are that it de-emphasized the need for intellectual excellence and that it ignored the structural realities of school.

The structural realities problem is to me the biggest flaw of the program. Simply put, why would you have a program that runs from grade 4 to grade 10 (the intermediate program) when kids change schools between grades 7 and 8? As Charles Ungerleider puts it, "You don't need a PhD in sociology to figure this out. It'll fail. They ignored the structural reality of separate buildings." To take this issue further, the length of the intermediate program also ignored the fact that kids in grade 10 are vastly different from kids in grade 4. By not at least stating that the intermediate program should differentiate between early and later years, the government made one of its biggest mistakes. "Covering a range of grade 4 to grade 10 is a huge scope," says Milt McClaren of SFU. "It encompasses students who in grade 4 are still children and in grade 10 they're not children anymore. Trying to put all that under an umbrella is extremely difficult in the first place."

In addition, the philosophy ignored the structure of classroom life. Stating that learning should be continuous and personalized is one thing: but how do teachers organize their classrooms to deal with twenty-five or more unique personal learning rates and styles? Defenders of the framework would likely respond by saying that this question would be answered in the program documents, that it was not the role of the framework to specify such fine details. My response would be that this is more than a fine detail. It's a big hole in the framework, an unfilled crack in the foundation, and without a solid foundation, a building falls. The Year 2000 framework assumed that a system organized like a factory—a time frame that obeys bells, a building divided into separate classrooms—could transform itself, even though it has been structured this way since the turn of the century. It ignored the fact that each classroom is led by a "supervisor" of sorts who has for an entire career been accustomed to controlling the flow of information. The framework needed to show how these people could change and this organizational structure could be reorganized.

Tom Fleming of U-Vic says Year 2000 "suggested" an intellectual softness, a lack of intellectual rigour. It's hard to find proof that Year 2000 was "close to anti-intellectual," as Fleming says. The strongest evidence is that the document does not emphasize academic excellence.

UBC's Charles Ungerleider stabs at it this way: Year 2000 indicated that teachers should be only a "guide on the side" and never a "sage on the stage." When this is manifested as less direct instruction by the teacher and more encouragement that the student pursue active learning, it's fine. But Ungerleider says the subtle suggestion of Year 2000 is that students need to learn everything on their own, without instruction. That is constructivism taken to an extreme: in some ways implying that every child must rediscover fire, must rediscover Newtonian physics. Ungerleider points out that the idea of teaching is to accelerate the learning process.

It could be argued that these—like many of the other criticisms of Year 2000—are criticisms of people's interpretation of the program, not of the program itself. But in fact, I agree that the framework philosophy did not emphasize academic excellence. Nor did it spell out concretely enough the precise nature of the teacher's role implied by constructivist philosophy. Therefore, it allowed misinterpretations to be made.

The misinterpretations of Year 2000 philosophy are what really sullied its reputation. Some teachers concluded that constructivism meant teachers can't teach kids anything, that they have to discover everything for themselves, even though the document did not say that. People thought Year 2000 meant they should never do any direct teaching, that all subjects must be integrated, and that they should teach kids skills and procedural knowledge without teaching them any content. Again, none of this was stated in Year 2000.

Two UBC administrators who sat on the steering committee that oversaw the team developing the graduation program, Olav Slaymaker and Jim Sherrill, argue that Year 2000 called for a whitewash of the status quo, replacing it with new techniques.

Slaymaker says a school system "shouldn't abandon tradition totally and put in something so radically different." Sherrill takes issue with throwing everything out and starting from scratch. Pointing out that B.C. is considered the best place in the English-speaking world to study math, he declares, "If something is working as well as math is, I don't want to touch it. The question we have to ask is, 'What's wrong with the system?' Year 2000 gave the impression that everything was wrong with the system. We threw out some 'God, mother, and apple pie' things."

Perhaps this is the problem with any revolution—the new regime dismisses everything about the old guard, including the good things about its philosophy. But a close look at the Year 2000 framework document shows that it did not encourage an overthrow of the old regime. It states clearly: students sometimes need to discuss and compare material with others, and "sometimes students learn best when they work individually"; teachers should use a wide range of teaching techniques and assessment methods; teachers "may wish to organize their teaching according to the traditional subjects or to clusters of subjects" in the intermediate program; they may include letter grades in report cards.

A FAILURE TO COMMUNICATE

So what happened? Why did Year 2000 become reviled across British Columbia? Why did people start to blame it for illiterate graduates and believe that it banned competition?

The beauty of the Year 2000 statement of learning principles was that every facet of an education program could be structured to reflect the principles. But the problem was that human beings were handed the task of structuring the programs and people's interpretation of principles can be fallible.

What occurred was a communication failure. The tale of miscommunication that is told over the next few chapters is at times comic, tragic, and epic. The screw-ups happened because of honest mistakes, deliberate disinformation, and a certain amount of ineptitude.

It reminds me of the game we all played when we were kids—my friends called it "Telephone," some call it "Secret Message." One person whispers a short passage to the next person in the circle, who in turn whispers to the next person his or her best recollection of what was said, and so on around the circle. In the end, we compare what the final person says to the original message and laugh at the difference. "In a restaurant by the river, a tall, blond man wearing a green hat told an old black woman that she left her umbrella beside the table" becomes "A black-haired man told the tall, blond woman that she left her umbrella under her chair in the restaurant," or something like that.

The lesson of the game is that communication is a two-way process: it involves one party transmitting material and another party receiving it. Errors in communication, in getting the message accurately from transmitter to receiver, can therefore be the fault of either party—perhaps the transmitter wasn't clear or the receiver did not understand. The problem is multiplied when the receiver then must turn his or her understanding of the message into a further communication. So when trying to find fault, we have to look at the parties on both ends of the transmitting-receiving chain.

The education reform communication chain worked like this: a Royal Commission transmitted its recommendations to government, then high-level employees of the government interpreted their understanding of the message and turned it into a further communication called "policy" (basically, *Policy Directions* and the Year 2000 framework document). Then lower-level employees of the government were charged with "implementing policy"—creating further documents designed to tell the front-line workers how to bring the policy to fruition. All of these transfers of information left plenty of room for miscommunication. In addition, a separate set of communications occurred off to the side of this top-down process: people in the public (media, voters) interpreted what they heard or read about policy and then communicated their version of it to others.

Communication problems are especially prone to happen with something as complex as education policy. If a Royal Commission says we should build a highway through a particular pass in the Cariboo Mountains, it's difficult to misinterpret that. But when the communication concerns such abstract ideas as principles of how people learn, it's ripe for misinterpretation.

It's worthwhile to examine the second stage in the communication process here. Earlier in this chapter, we looked at whether the government's *Policy Directions* paper accurately reflected the Royal Commission report. The question to ask now is whether *Year 2000: A Framework for Learning* accurately reflected the policy paper and the intentions of the Royal Commission.

Wayne Desharnais, then assistant deputy minister for finance, says the government was very careful in ensuring that policy reflected the Royal Commission. "I met with Royal Commission staff, people like Terry McBurney and Tarry Grieve and Tom Fleming, and they were really pleased that the government had actually listened and was doing a lot of what was recommended in the report," he says.

But as stated in the last chapter, many people feel that somewhere along the way, Year 2000 (including the program documents that were to follow) subverted the intent of the Royal Commission. "The biggest leap in logic" during the whole process was from the Royal Commission to the Year 2000 discussion paper, says Jim Sherrill, UBC's associate dean of education. "Once that first document came out, we were headed down the path."

The Royal Commission report was "forward-looking and responding to very specific concerns, but when the Year 2000 came out, other agendas were put forward," says UBC's Olav Slaymaker. He says the Sullivan commission called for excellence in education and was a bottom-up process. He accuses the Education Ministry of making the Year 2000 top-down and simplifying the Royal Commission into a progressive ideology. "The very strong emphasis on long-term competitiveness in the Sullivan report was lost in the ministry's evaluation of it."

Those who served on the Royal Commission have definite opinions as well, but can't say for sure what happened. "Things moved farther and farther away from the Royal Commission but exactly how it was done or why it was done, I don't know," says David Robitaille, another UBC education professor who served as one of the Royal Commission research directors. "We weren't a part of the Year 2000 process at all. I was on the sidelines observing what they were doing, wringing my hands from time to time."

Valerie Overgaard, who served under Robitaille on the curriculum research team, says she thought it odd that nobody from the ministry contacted them to clarify ideas or make sure their interpretation was right. She says the ministry took good ideas from the Royal Commission and mandated them in a rigid way. "Whereas we said it would be a good idea for kids to connect what they're learning in one area with other areas, the ministry said curriculum will be integrated," says Overgaard. "The difference between those things is huge." She adds that the notion of child-centred learning is antithetical to the liberal education promoted by the Royal Commission. "Our fundamental point throughout is that the first ten years of schooling should be based on the notion of a broad liberal education." She acknowledges, however, that the Royal Commission was somewhat vague and general enough that people could find things in it to justify particular standpoints.

Tarry Grieve says the implementation of Year 2000 included "many ideas that had nothing to do with the Royal Commission and they were the most controversial." For instance, he cited the concept that teachers shouldn't write report cards that tell kids the truth about how they're doing because it might be destructive to them.

How the Royal Commission recommendations became Year 2000 is "probably one of the mysteries of the whole process," says Robin Brayne, North Vancouver district superintendent and co-author of the research report on teachers. "What transpired between the recommendations being promulgated to the government and the document coming out on the Year 2000 itself is anybody's guess." He argues that very little in the Royal Commission spoke to curriculum. The parts that did said the curriculum is for the most part sound and doesn't need massive overhaul but some areas do need attention, especially relevance for those not going to university. Consequently, he was surprised that Year 2000 was driven by curriculum organization. The division of the grades into primary, intermediate, and graduation programs and the emphasis on the principles of learning, integration, continuous progress, and co-operative learning weren't prominent in the Royal Commission, says Brayne.

Arthur Kratzmann, the number two man on the commission, differs from his colleagues. "I've heard people say that [the Year 2000 differed from the commission], but I've never seen documentation of what they really meant," says Kratzmann, "I didn't see too much change of emphasis."

Elmer Froese, Burnaby superintendent and another senior researcher on the commission, falls somewhere in between. He says Year 2000 curriculum recommendations were based on the Royal Commission but were in some cases a definite aberration of the commission's intent. More important to Froese was the Education Ministry's misinterpretation of process and governance recommendations. (This is dealt with in the next chapter as part of the bigger picture surrounding implementation of policy.)

The conventional wisdom in the B.C. education community today is that the Royal Commission was good and Year 2000 was a bad and unfortunate glitch in the process, but the system is now back on track. This conclusion is flawed. Year 2000 was a logical response to the recommendations of the Royal Commission. The glitch came later: in the interpretation of Year 2000 philosophy by ministry staff, teachers, and the public.

One of the reasons Year 2000 was considered to be problematic is that it called for fundamental changes to the system. People who served on the Royal Commission say they did not call for big reforms. "We said we didn't see a need for wholesale change. We saw lots of good things happening and we wanted to support more of them," says Valerie Overgaard of the curriculum research team. "We were fairly realistic about how much change there could be. If you just support teachers to make differences in small ways throughout the province then the already good things that are happening are going to spread even more. I don't think we thought that we were going to revolutionize or in any way make huge wholesale changes."

The Royal Commission didn't use the words "fundamental change" but the fact remains that it drew a portrait of a changing society that indicated the need for fundamental changes. It's true that the Royal Commission recommended periodic adjustment in education policy rather than widespread reform. Yet there's a contradiction that the Royal Commission report did not acknowledge: the kind of system it envisaged would in fact be widely different from the status quo. The Royal Commission outlined major changes in society, pointed to business demands for creative thinkers and problem-solvers, emphasized the need to teach students skills, not just knowledge. Consequently, the task the Royal Commission set before the education system demanded a certain amount of revolution. Remember, this is a system that is more remarkable for its similarities to what it was like in the 1940s than for its differences. Look in the typical grade 10 classroom and the scene—except for the clothes the kids are wearing and the racial backgrounds—is the same as any classroom from forty or fifty years ago. A big desk in the front, a blackboard with notes on it, smaller desks in rows facing forward, bored kids slumping in their seats in the back, and a teacher who talks for 80 percent of the class time. The Royal Commission said teachers should use an interdisciplinary approach throughout all years of the common curriculum (grades 1 to 10); it encouraged experimenting with multigrade classrooms; it said, "The final years of the common curriculum should resemble the model of the elementary schools rather than the model of the present junior secondary school." If this is not a call for fundamental changes from the status quo, what is?

Some who served on the Royal Commission have tried to divorce their recommendations from what followed because they didn't want to be dragged down with the failure of Year 2000. The program's flaws stemmed more from those implementing the program than those who formulated the philosophical guidelines. Royal Commission staff should not feel the need to deny responsibility.

SFU professor Roland Case, a member of the intermediate program steering committee, has a theory that the problems with Year 2000 stem from two areas: the way that principles were articulated and the way they were implemented. He says Year 2000 articulated such "vague grand principles" as "putting kids at the centre" in ways that did not allow proper program planning or development. In turn, this "prevented any thoughtful implementation because there never was that level of clarity as to what these things could and shouldn't be. Even though some people understood it, so many of the people in the ministry and elsewhere didn't understand it and there were conflicting understandings." As a result, says Case, "Many speakers would go around and instead of saying like I would, 'These are really complex things, we've got to do our homework, we've got to be rigorous, we've got to be hard-nosed about this,' they would be saying, 'Look you know who your kids are, you know what works best for you, just trust your intuitions, go talk about it, think about it and then do it.' The implication that it was hard work and would require considerable study and inquiring and that it might mean challenging some of your fundamental intuitions about what was important was not promoted."

On the front lines, this caused teachers to misinterpret Year 2000 philosophy, argues Case. He says one reason is that teachers tend not to appreciate the theory behind the practice of teaching. "The large numbers of teachers seemed concerned only with, 'Don't tell me why we have to do it, just tell me what you want me to do.' Unless you understand the principles and the rationale behind these ideas then the chances of them being misapplied are obvious."

For example, teachers misunderstood the principle of active learning. "Lots of people even to this day think that meant getting kids out of their seats more," says Case, "having kids manipulate their hands, playing with something, doing something, that sitting there thinking was not active."

Charles Ungerleider, UBC's associate dean of teacher education, also says some teachers misunderstood some of the ideas behind Year 2000, including active learning. He cites more examples. For instance, some tried to force all their teaching into themes, the idea that integration would be achieved by relating every subject to a single issue like dinosaurs. "If we didn't have dinosaurs, we wouldn't have grade 2," he says, only somewhat facetiously. In addition, many teachers had the sense they were supposed to abandon the teaching of phonics and opt for the whole-language approach (the idea that reading and writing should be taught through the context and meaning of stories). But nowhere did Year 2000 endorse whole-language over phonics.

Like a child who rushes out the door to school without eating breakfast, who is ignored by teachers, and whose parents give no encouragement to do homework, the Year 2000 reforms were bound to fail. The next chapters tell the story of how that happened.

1. Quoted in *Vancouver Sun*, October 13, 1989.

2. Decima Research, "Strategic Communications Study," unpublished document, July, 30, 1988, p. 12.

3. Ibid., p. 16.

4. Ibid., p. 17.

5. Ibid., p. 19.

6. "Major Changes to Education Announced," B.C. Ministry of Education, news release 06-89, January 27, 1989.

7. Ronald Marx and Tarrance Grieve, *The Learners of British Columbia*, 1988, p. 95.

8. Ibid., pp. 84–95 and p. 111.

9. Ibid., p. 92.

[4]
BALLOONS AND BAPTIST REVIVAL MEETINGS:
1989 - 1991

On the first day of school in September 1989, Saanich district superintendent Janet Mort filled the elevators of the Education Ministry building with balloons. That's just one of the reasons why Mort is described by various people as entrepreneurial, flamboyant, and sensationalist—anything but dull. She evokes many responses, but never indifference. Mort was recruited in May 1989 to run the new "innovations branch" of the ministry. This branch was deputy minister Sandy Peel's idea for marketing Year 2000, first to the field then to parents and the public.

"She's a motivator. She could bring a team of teachers together and it was wonderful to watch," says Peel. "She could rub some people the wrong way, there's no question about that. On the other hand, she knew how to sell, she knew how to get these things out there, she knew how to fire people up and get them committed. She knew how to communicate."

And, having become a principal at twenty-two and a superintendent at thirty-nine, Mort is not given to false modesty. During my conversation with her in her home overlooking Brentwood Bay, she says such things as "I write really well," "There are a lot of people who would pay to send kids to the kind of school I would design," and "I had had a reputation as an innovator for all my career. Way back in the early seventies I won a BCTF award for innovation. Saanich became known in the eight years I was there as being one of the most progressive districts in the province, it was acknowledged by everybody."

When Mort started work at the ministry, Peel called forty people into a meeting, introduced her, and told the gathered crowd, "Your job is to do what she needs you to do." Mort was given status equal to that of an assistant deputy minister, reporting directly to Peel, putting a few noses out of joint. Peel told her to spend the summer planning the marketing campaign that would begin in the fall. She was given a $6-million budget for year one.

"He really left me on my own but he gave me two instructions. He said number one I was to light fires all over the province. My job was to get people excited about the Year 2000. He had no idea about how I should go about doing it, but that was my job. And then the other one was to put out the brush fires. Where there was resistance, I was to keep the resistance down."

THE $6-MILLION SALES PITCH

Peel and Mort chose principals and teachers as the main focus of their marketing campaign. This meant they were bypassing superintendents, who saw education reform as their turf, generating some hostility in the process. To this day, superintendents bristle at the mention of Janet Mort. But her innovations branch could do what it wanted because it held certain purse-strings. It had $3 million to dole out for "teacher interaction," a kind of professional development to get staff talking about the Year 2000 changes. The ministry "targeted" this money—rather than just giving it to districts to throw into the general pot, superintendents had to spend it as dictated. Mort's philosophy was, "The only way this change would occur is if teachers became engaged in designing how it would happen in their classrooms."

The real thrust for pushing Year 2000 began in the fall of 1989 with eight regional meetings with 2,800 principals and vice-principals across the province, at a cost of $1 million. Says Mort, "The research had said that school administrators could get in the way of the change and stop it if they chose to. If you didn't get them on side, that's what would occur. Our purpose was to make sure they felt informed."

The result was day-long, multi-media presentations that had the atmosphere of tent revival meetings—balloons, multiple video screens,

Whitney Houston singing "The Greatest Love of All." In the morning, a big-screen, rear-projection slide show with Mort narrating featured a young girl named Katie. Entitled "Why Change?", Mort's forty-five-minute speech "wasn't about education. It was about the world changing. It was about the changes in health, the changes in demographics, politics, the environment. I appealed to emotion. I've always used emotion in my speeches because it's a way that you get people to feel something, No matter what it is they're feeling, they at least become engaged."

Mort spoke of what the world would be like for Katie in 2000 (the year, not the program) as she made her way through school: that 94 percent of jobs would require post-secondary education, she would face five career changes, would need to retrain every five to seven years. "I was talking to people who didn't want to believe that, didn't want to know about it. What I was doing was confronting them with the reality of where kids are going and what they're going to have to face and then challenged them in the speech with, 'So who's going to help them get there? It's us, folks. You and me, because there's nobody else that's going to prepare them for that.' "

After Mort's speech, the three teams would describe their programs to the principals. And after lunch, Jack Fleming, assistant deputy minister responsible for Year 2000, delivered his keynote speech explaining why the program proposals would begin to address the challenges Mort mentioned in the morning.

Mort admits the show was not always well received. Shouting matches broke out, people argued that there was no need for change and that the government could not make them change.

"We had one meeting where people were yelling at the back of the room. We had one in Vancouver where people got up at microphones and raged and ranted about my panel on the stage," says Mort. "There'd be a lot of people who didn't like it, but I didn't mind. They didn't like it because we were forcing them to look at something they didn't want to look at."

To the criticism that the presentations spoke more to emotion than intellect and had more style than substance, Mort answers, "Yes, they did try to appeal to people on an emotional level. There's a lot of emotion attached to the lives of children. . . . You have to provide forums for feelings. You can't make change in organizations in a major way unless you provide people with the opportunity to vent, so that was what we were doing. Our effort was not to persuade them, our effort was to engage them in talking about their feelings.

"We woke this province up," she says. "For a lot of people in the province, it was permission to celebrate; permission to celebrate children and what we could do. The positive people, the people who wanted to move forward and who have always wanted to move forward, we released them, we validated them."

"It certainly captured people's attention, there's no doubt about that," says Jack Fleming. "People have never forgotten the initiation of the Year 2000." Fleming admits that the presentations weren't perfect and that some people resented them, but he thinks they were the right thing to do. "If an intellectual exercise was all it was going to take to sell it, it would have sold itself. But it wasn't about to do that because many educators simply hadn't kept up with research about how programs might be designed to help kids learn, things like that. We really got stagnated in the eighties because all the attention was on money, bargaining, legislation, fighting with the government."

But many educators felt the Mort road show put them on the receiving end of hoopla rather than thoughtful substance, persuasion and sales pitches rather than carefully laid out process. Some people felt the innovations branch was trying to market Year 2000 like soap.

Program Teams

If the innovations branch was the ministry's marketing arm for Year 2000, the research and developmental arms were the three teams developing the primary, intermediate, and graduation programs. It's essential to understand the importance of the program teams to the events that follow. Out of view of the public, reporting directly to independent advisory committees and therefore somewhat at arm's length from the Education Ministry, these were the little-known think-tanks that shaped the direction of education reform in B.C.

The three program development teams were made up of five to seven staff from the field. A "team leader" was picked from each of these. The ministry provided support people and a couple of senior staff to act as managers or directors, but the programs were to be generated by the teams. Overseeing each team was a "steering committee," each made up of about eighteen people representing the interest groups (BCTF, BCSTA, principals, superintendents, parents, business, labour, etc.) The teams were to report to the steering committees for feedback on their work.

The teams were a new concept in the ministry. Ministry branches had always been responsible for developing curriculum and assessment guides. In the past, teachers and principals had been seconded to these branches to help develop curriculum, but the task remained firmly in the hands of the ministry. Program teams made up entirely of out-siders—and reporting to outside advisory committees—were a first. Sources say it created a certain amount of tension on Superior Street because ministry staff envied the power and freedom of the team members.

But more importantly, the people on the teams weren't prepared for the task they faced on the larger scale. In theory, they were charged with developing education programs, which was easy enough, since the people hired were considered some of the best educators in the province. But in reality, they also needed to get teachers, principals, and the public to go along with the changed education program, a much tougher task.

Says Burnaby superintendent Elmer Froese, "Virtually none of them had any experience with massive large-scale change. Most of them had never been anything other than a classroom teacher. Designing what was being characterized as one of the biggest lead-ing-edge changes in public education in the western world was in the hands of people who understood teaching and learning ex-tremely well, but the process of change not very well."

Tom Fleming says the team members were well-intentioned but not very analytical, "a bunch of folks who all of a sudden had been given the keys to the candy store: 'You can make the education system the way you want.' To make things simple takes a really long time. The folks inside never had that kind of clarity of vision. They built things with bells and whistles. When you're spending buckets of money, sooner or later someone's going to come along and say, 'Can I have a look at the fenders? How fast will it go?'"

A member of one of the steering committees says the teams were made up of "a bunch of people whose passion just took over." Staffed with independent minds, the teams took on a power and life of their own, pushing things in what he thinks was a much more radical and progressive way than necessary. "The group became this evangelistic core of saviours of the system and anyone who had any objection just didn't understand it," he says. "There were those who agreed, who had the spirit and the vision of the Year 2000, and then there was the enemy. I remember being made to feel like a traitor and like scum because I was raising questions, con-cerns, issues around these things. There was no room for anything other than wild enthusiasm. Any critical voice was seen to be hostile."

The amount of faith put into the teams is an anomaly. Normally the bureaucracy is highly centralized and dictatorial, yet it gave the teams a high degree of creative freedom. It left the outcomes of the programs almost entirely to these few people plucked from among the thousands of educators in the province. Their unique personalities shaped the programs they developed.

The all-woman primary team was established in March 1989. Its members were Marilyn Chapman, Julie Davis, Joan Hall, Jackie Link, Janis Johnson, Marlene Dergousoff, and Colleen Politano. Johnson, Dergousoff, and Politano returned for the second phase of the program development in 1990 and were joined by Lois Blackmore, Kathleen Dahlstrom, and Luanne Whiles. Observers say this group was unified in its vision and got along with each other. Some of them had been involved in the BCTF's primary teachers provincial specialist association (including Hall, a former association president) while others (such as Politano and Dergousoff) worked on curriculum revisions and technique guides and gave professional development workshops to their fellow teachers. The team worked quickly, issuing its draft program document in June 1989, less than four months after starting work.

The intermediate team was a more diverse group, spanning the grades from 4 to 10 and representing a variety of educational approaches. It started off with nine members, only three of whom stayed on the team until it disbanded in 1993—math teacher Phil Foster from Cranbrook, science teacher Graham Hunter from Sooke, and elementary school principal Daphne Morris from Saanich. Morris (who later changed her name to Daphne Macnaughton) took over in 1991 from team leader Dave Gulley, principal of Lloyd George Elementary in Kamloops. The group was highly influenced by the primary team and its ideas, and over time, the members of the group moved toward a more child-centred focus.

The original members of the male-dominated graduation team were team leader Dave Watkins, principal of Victoria High School; Gordon Shead, another principal from Castlegar; teachers John Fitzgibbon from the South Okanagan district and Peter Savage of Chilliwack; and Bobby Gill, a Camosun College instructor.

The staff in the ministry who selected the intermediate team members in 1989 weren't the same people who selected the graduation team the same year, and the different compositions revealed themselves over the years. At times, sparks flew between the two teams. The intermediate team didn't want its program to be driven by the graduation program, but the graduation team felt the intermediate program wouldn't prepare kids well enough for the final two years of school. To this day, there's a grudge-like friction in the voices of members of each team when they talk about the other.

"We chose to disagree much of the time, to be candid with you," says graduation team leader Dave Watkins. "We were quite dissimilar in our views of things." He says the intermediate team members carried their constructivist view of learning so far that tunnel vision was the result. "I felt they should have been far more consistent with the views of Sullivan," he says. "If you didn't want to build upon Sullivan . . . you built on the personal individual views of the members of the team. The moment you do that you're on quicksand in terms of a foundation. [The graduation team] could always defend our arguments that we were consistent with Sullivan."

The graduation team members fell more in line with the bureaucratic mould, says the intermediate team's Phil Foster. "We weren't people that followed orders well."

There's a temptation to point to personalities as one of the reasons why the program documents took their particular bent. There's no doubt that team members had educational biases but there's also a danger in overstating the importance of individuals and their characteristics.

Some problems can be traced to the ministry giving little direction to the teams. They knew they were supposed to produce program documents, but what was their reference point? A ministry staffer tells me the Year 2000 document was designed to be the "solid professional framework to guide the work of the teams" in making their programs reflect two key anchor points: the Royal Commission, plus current research literature on measurement systems, accountability, curriculum design, and the ways that kids learn.

But Dave Watkins says the Royal Commission alone was always the graduation team's beacon. "Our role was to design a program with a good deal of independence from the bureaucracy in the ministry . . . more in consultation with our steering committee," he says. "We kind of drifted away from the ministry bureaucracy and became more responsive to the graduation steering committee."

SANDY PEEL'S DEPARTURE

On October 12, 1989, in the middle of Janet Mort's marketing campaign, the supporters of Year 2000 suffered a serious blow when the government plucked Sandy Peel from his deputy minister position in education to head the Forest Resources Commission. It seems the Socreds felt they'd defused the controversy that was education, and facing bigger battles in the woods, they called in the successful troubleshooter. But it left a void in education.

"It's unfortunate in a sense I got pulled out of education. I wanted at least another year to get the whole process better cemented," says Peel. Had he stayed longer, he says he would have ensured that Mort's public relations campaign went into schools and would have worked on "better explanation [of Year 2000] to all the people out there, particularly to the parents."

"Sandy knew exactly what he was doing and I think the Year 2000 wouldn't have run into the trouble it did if Sandy had stayed 'cause he was the force behind it," says Mort.

Charles Ungerleider calls Sandy Peel's transfer the government's fundamental mistake. After Peel left, he says, "The momentum behind Year 2000 seemed blunted." Peel had a specific strategy for change and understood the process of change.

The difficult task of stepping into Sandy Peel's shoes fell to Wayne Desharnais, who had been assistant deputy minister responsible for finance and administration since 1987. Desharnais had been with the ministry for ten years, starting out in charge of special education and becoming executive director of field services in 1985. Before coming to Victoria, Desharnais was a secondary-school principal and director of special programs in Prince George. Some observers say Desharnais didn't have Peel's forcefulness nor—more importantly—his commitment to Year 2000. Critics say he neither agreed with nor understood Peel's strategy for change, didn't push the program when he appeared before cabinet, de-emphasized the high-profile marketing tactics of the innovations branch.

Sandy Peel says his replacement was in a difficult position as acting deputy minister for the first five months and "wasn't prepared to stand up and take some of the rough flak around this thing."

But today, Desharnais comes across as a staunch defender of Year 2000. "It's been made clear that there needs to be fundamental reform to the public school system if it's going to survive," says Desharnais, adding that he felt Year 2000, although it had its flaws, was the kind of fundamental reform required.

He's critical of some of the mistakes the government made in trying to implement it during his tenure. He didn't like Janet Mort's use of balloons and would have preferred "good, solid documentation" and straight talk. "I think in some cases the innovations (branch) side got carried away," says Desharnais. "That to me was the wrong kind of PR and marketing and communications."

He also feels the government should have done a better job explaining the program to the public. "This was a really big, complex thing that was costing a lot of money" and therefore it had to be explained to the populace, says Desharnais. "The general communications with the public left something to be desired." He says the idea of spending money on explaining Year 2000 to the public came under a lot of scrutiny at Treasury Board and wasn't welcomed warmly.

First Drafts of Intermediate and Graduation Programs

Tony Brummet released the first drafts of the intermediate and graduation programs at the BCSTA annual general meeting in April 1990. The intermediate program binder was a whopping 252 pages, plus a 14-page response form. The graduation program draft was thinner—98 pages, plus 6 pages for response. It's impossible to summarize the content of such large documents in a few paragraphs—the interested reader should consult the originals—but a few key points can be made.

INTERMEDIATE PROGRAM The intermediate program draft followed the spirit of Year 2000 but took it even further. The most useful section for understanding the intermediate program—and for getting a sense of its flaws—is part two of the six-part booklet. In it, the program made a variety of "position statements" that were based on Year 2000 principles yet had a prescriptive tone to them. The position statements were pitched in stark contrast to current education practice, implying that the existing system needed to be tossed away completely. This was not the goal of the Year 2000 framework, but the intermediate team said things that made the status quo sound just plain evil. On integration: "Isolating one subject from another, creating separate subjects within subjects, and specifying discrete learnings within each subject has given rise to disintegration of personal learning and fragmentation of school experiences." On letter grades: "The use of letter grades is perhaps the single biggest aspect of schooling that affects students' self-esteem and their ultimate success in the system." On continuous progress: "Comparing student development to prescribed learning objectives and ranking progress in relation to others is not the purpose of a continuous progress system."

These three statements alone show the intermediate team's misinterpretation of Year 2000 principles and show how they appeared to forbid teachers from using any of the techniques they'd used throughout their careers. The team should not have portrayed traditional practices as venal: the fact is it's not a sin to teach some material from one subject alone on occasion; calling letter grades the single biggest impact on self-esteem is hyperbole; and if a student's progress isn't compared to learning objectives, what use is it in having objectives in the first place? The intermediate program team should not have characterized everything from the past as bad: they should have started from the premise that some things work in existing practice, asking fellow educators to build on those good things and fix what doesn't work.

Today, few people in education have anything good to say about the intermediate program. Valerie Overgaard of the Vancouver school district says the program almost totally neglected curriculum. "Everything was process, no content."

Says one of the Royal Commission researchers, "Those guys were out to lunch. A lot of half-baked ideas. They just weren't realistic at all."

North Vancouver superintendent Robin Brayne says the program "was educator talk, created by educators for educators, complete with eduspeak, very, very broad correct statements but not the kind of statements that one could sort of translate into any sort of systemic reform." He says the program failed to answer basic questions: What will change? Will curriculum change? Will the style of instruction change? Will school organization change? "What they didn't build on it were changes to the stuff of schools, what is taught to students. The how was talked about, how to organize, learning principles, but nothing about the what."

"The intermediate program draft really didn't talk much about what it is we expect kids to learn," says a ministry bureaucrat. "It talked a lot about the theory of learning and teaching, that kind of stuff. It was more of a statement of philosophy of what happened in schools."

One member of the intermediate steering committee begged the team not to distribute the immense first draft. "If we sent out a document that was as woolly as that one was and as big as that one was, it wouldn't be read and it would be misunderstood. I remember having tears in my eyes and pleading with them, 'Please don't do it,' because I believed there was so much of value there that would be lost unless they could lay it out more clearly."

Knowing now what she didn't know then, team leader Daphne Macnaughton admits the document needed to be fixed. "If going back and changing the language to be more practical, to be something that more people could connect with, if that would have led to a different result, then I would do that. Would I compromise the values that we laid out? Never."

Today, it's hard to find people willing to admit that they agreed with the intermediate program. But in fact, the overall response in the field to the philosophy of the intermediate program was positive.

After the draft was released in the spring of 1990, the ministry asked for feedback. The following year, once the response came in, the ministry hired Arnold Toutant Consulting Group to analyse the reaction. The report said, "The majority of the field supports the intentions of the Intermediate Program." By analysing the 3,526 responses received, the consultant showed that only 10 percent were opposed, noting that most of those opposed believed the current system was fine.

However, the support for the intermediate program was not without its conditions. In the main, concerns were raised about implementing the program and about clarity of the terms. The report said the major challenge for the intermediate team would be addressing the field's concerns about assessment, evaluation, and reporting. "Although people agreed that there is a need to improve students' self-esteem, many respondents said that 'can-do' reporting may not provide complete or honest communication," said the report. It also noted that the proposed "reconsideration" of letter grades drew a vast difference of opinion—some wanted them banned outright, others wanted them left in. Respondents also worried about the workload involved in the proposed assessment techniques.

In its recommendations, the report said the intermediate document should include concrete descriptions and examples of key elements of the program (like continuous progress and integration) to ensure that people understand what they are and what they aren't. The report recommended extensive editorial changes to the document (glossary, index, research excerpts, photographs, and graphics). It also pointed to the need for the team to work closely with skilled writing and production staff.

The report also included a long list of recommendations for the ministry: give educators information and practical suggestions on how to approach change; improve the understanding of the program changes among parents and the community, including increased media coverage; answer staff's biggest concerns about implementing the program—professional development, funding, and time.

Reading this review, it's clear that the majority accepted the philosophy and intentions of the program. At the same time they were telling the team and the ministry they had work to do. Teachers were saying, "Yes, we like this program, but you ought to answer these questions and ensure these things are done first."

GRADUATION PROGRAM   The draft laid out the program in two components—general studies, to be taken by all, and selected options. The five option programs were called university, career-preparation, community-school partnership, passport to apprenticeship, and exploration. The traditional year-long "course" or subject was divided into four "units" in an effort to increase flexibility: students would be able to choose only one or two units of courses and perhaps five or six others.

General studies was the graduation program's attempt at integration. It consisted of twelve units (the equivalent of three full-year courses) encompassing the goals of grade 11 social studies, English, and science.

In "selected options" (forty units) all students were required to take the four units each of grade 12 English and grade 11 math. A further twenty units (the equivalent of five courses) were to be related to a student's post-secondary plans, with twelve units (three courses) as free electives. Depending on the option selected, requirements for work experience varied (from one unit [about twenty-five hours] for students in the university program to eight units for those in the community-school partnership option).

In its ninety-eight pages, the draft managed to anticipate many of the questions that staff would ask: it included a section acknowledging implementation issues, a five-page glossary, samples of report cards and student self-assessment forms, and sections on special issues like ESL and special-needs students.

The graduation program draft received less flak, mainly because it was structured to respond to already specified graduation requirements. Because of this dictate, the program said assessment must judge performance "in relation to a set standard." Otherwise, a diploma would be meaningless.

However, David Robitaille, head of the Royal Commission's curriculum research team, says the graduation program made political errors by talking about integration and de-emphasizing the academic side of school without ensuring they had universities on side. "They got a lot of heat that they didn't really need. Part of the reason the thing failed had to do with strategies. They should have made sure that the constituent groups were on side."

UBC's Faculties of Arts and Science took swipes at the graduation program in reports released in 1990. Although the Faculty of Arts committee recognized the virtues of Year 2000 for students who don't continue in university, the committee wrote that it "feels very serious misgivings with respect to the implications for university-bound students." The report said the graduation program "undermines the traditional disciplines" and "erodes attempts to achieve academic excellence"; its heavy emphasis on the student denies the importance of teacher and parents; its portrayal of the university option as one of five equally desirable paths "does a disservice to students and may damage the economic future of the province"; increased disparity between public and private schools could result from the emphasis on allowing students to progress at their own rate; and the massive changes to the style of education would require radical revamping of teacher-education programs and an infusion of more money.

In June 1991, the ministry sponsored a colloquium at Whistler that Wayne Desharnais says was an attempt to get support from the university community. A good sample of response to the graduation program is contained in the summary report from the colloquium, which lists six guidelines for the graduation team and the ministry in developing the next version of the program. At the top of the list, colloquium participants—who also included representatives from business lobby groups—wanted the program's purposes and emphases clarified more distinctly. Is it about attaining academic excellence or reducing the drop-out rate, about serving the needs of students or meeting the economic needs of the province? Participants found the program ambiguous on such issues as integration vs. disciplinary studies and teaching content vs. process. The second recommendation demanded a re-examination of the shift from intermediate to graduation program. Participants were concerned with the "philosophical lurch" from the developmental learning of the intermediate program to the standards-focused approach of the graduation program. The colloquium asked the ministry to re-examine curriculum content and give further thought to the idea that certain subjects should be retained. The three other recommendations asked the ministry to allow sufficient time for program development and implementation, explain the program's financial implications, and clarify the political and public commitment to the program.

Although he was in charge of program development, Jack Fleming says it wasn't a big deal to him that the first draft documents had problems. From his perspective, they were preliminary versions designed to launch a philosophical debate, so the fact that they were neither elegant nor fine-tuned was irrelevant. "In the beginning, if we'd come out with a highly articulated framework for the intermediate and grad levels, people could have very rightly criticized us for having invented those things out of thin air. And yes, they were rambly and even the teams weren't happy with them. They were creatures of committees and there was a lot of work to be done. But it wasn't a problem in my sense. The bigger problem was to get people into the dialogue. That was the biggest issue. From a tactical, strategic point of view, being in charge of the whole thing, my largest problem was to persuade the partner groups that this was a serious effort at change, that they should spend some time and energy on it. Coming from an era when there had been no collaboration, rather downright distrust, the notion that you could sit down and have a philosophical discussion about this was just foreign."

However, critics of the programs wanted more than philosophical discussions. The drafts were criticized as lacking specifics on assessment and giving the impression that standards were being abandoned. Fleming accepts that the documents were thin on assessment, but adds that the ministry thought it would have more time to fill in the gaps before the heat began.

One of the reasons there were gaps was the short time frame the government gave to the teams. The intermediate and graduation teams were put together in the summer of 1989 and they produced the first drafts by the following April. The Socreds were in a hurry-up offence, wanting something tangible to show they were taking action. "There was a lot of political pressure to produce something," says graduation team leader Dave Watkins. "We were pressured to produce a draft fairly quickly, way too quickly." He admits that the document was rather vague and included a lot of words that meant nothing, but points out that the team was in a learning process.

Says Jack Fleming, "I'm not absolutely sure that that's the way we really should have begun but it was the old government edict, 'You've got to get something done in a short time line, you've got to get framework documents out there so people can come to an understanding, come to grips with this.'"

"The field simply did not know how to handle draft documents or proposals," adds Watkins. "People weren't used to getting something that was in a draft form to which they would respond with input."

In addition, the field wasn't familiar with the concept of a document that spelled out a program philosophy as opposed to a given subject curriculum. "We had a lot of trouble over our four years in terms of talking to educators about the concept of a program as opposed to a course or a curriculum," says Graham Hunter of the intermediate team. "Here we were talking about a program which encompasses curriculum, assessment, instruction, everything."

THE DUAL-ENTRY FIASCO

In the 1990–91 school year, the first visible reform to the school system was made mandatory: dual-entry kindergarten. Kids who turned five by the end of October could start school in September, those who turned five in November through the following April were to start in January.

The theory behind dual entry was sound. Research shows that the twelve-month age range among kids who are so young makes for vastly different levels of development in a given kindergarten class: some kids are five years and nine months old while others are four years and nine months old; some kids have just given up their pacifiers while others can print the alphabet. It's been well proven by research that the younger kids are more likely to fail in the early years of school. It's not because they're stupid but because they haven't developed to the level of their peers. The idea of dual entry was to reduce the range of development levels in each kindergarten class. The idea had its genesis in the Royal Commission recommendation that the system accept kids for school entrance not on the basis of chronological age but their level of development.

Although the theory was sound, little attention was paid to details: public reaction, for one. Naturally, since starting school in September ranks with death and taxes in people's psyches as one of the few certainties in life, dual entry upset many parents, especially those whose kids were born in November and December. They had a sense their children were being left behind. The government didn't do enough proper explanation of the reasons for dual entry, nor did it answer people's questions of how it would work in practice.

But more importantly, the government had not conceived of the end product of dual entry. It implies a need for dual exit points: if a child started the four-year primary program in January, wouldn't he or she likely exit it in December four years later? These questions were unanswered.

Dual entry was hastily conceived and hastily thrown together. Politics is the reason. The Socreds wanted to look decisive. An election was around the corner. A senior bureaucrat puts it this way: "Government's feeling was that [dual entry] would stimulate change in the system, it would be a visible and immediate step." Translation: government wanted the voters to notice that it was acting on its education reform promises. This was a government that—facing political scandals galore—desperately wanted to be popular. So the political masters put pressure on ministry staff to enact something tangible in a hurry.

The government wasn't helped by a number of school districts that either dragged their heels on dual entry or else complained vociferously about it. The BCTF also opposed it from the start. "Right from the beginning we said this isn't going to work, it's impractical, and it should be abandoned," says then-president Ken

Novakowski. "We were very loud and clear about that publicly and otherwise, making presentations to the ministry and the minister." He continues, "The dual-entry fiasco . . . told us that caution when you're dealing with half a million school children and their lives is an appropriate factor in everything we do. We shouldn't jump into things because they look good. We need to know they're good and that they're going to work."

Burnaby superintendent Elmer Froese says dual entry is philosophically sound but was implemented poorly. Flexible entry would have been the natural outcome of a few years of applying the principle that students develop at different rates. Instead, "The policy makers and senior officials accepted the fact of change by edict, which is a complete and total contradiction of the very principle they were implementing. No one was ready for it. Even the bureaucratic mechanisms were not ready, much less the developmental ones. Even the record-keeping wasn't there."

The rumblings of discontent among some parents and teachers about the screw-ups surrounding dual entry set the whole Year 2000 reform off in the wrong direction. Dual entry caught people's attention and according to polls, its problems became linked with Year 2000 in the public's mind.

Perhaps, had the ministry kept sailing with dual entry, the question of exit points would have been answered, the public would have become accustomed to January entrance, and the controversy would have died down. But the death of dual entry was written on the wall when the other half of the dynamic duo, Tony Brummet, announced in December 1990 that he would not seek re-election and Premier Vander Zalm ejected him from cabinet.

STAN HAGEN

Stan Hagen, formerly minister of Advanced Education and Economic Development, took over for Brummet. He was an interesting choice to run the public school system: Hagen attended Lutheran college and university and two of his five children weren't attending public schools, rather Christian private schools. It seemed that he was merely a caretaker education minister until the election, which had to be called in less than a year. But Hagen immediately began sending signs that he was not too happy with either dual entry or Year 2000 as a whole.

Hagen's contacts were in the post-secondary field and he was no doubt influenced by their opinions of Year 2000, says then-deputy minister Wayne Desharnais. But he adds, "I think [Hagen] did see it as something that was going to work as long as the standards were there."

Assistant deputy minister Jack Fleming says Hagen wasn't as committed to Year 2000, was quizzical about it, and didn't really understand it. "While he didn't object to it, he wasn't wildly supportive of it," says Fleming. To compound matters, the rest of the government was starting to have second thoughts on some of the specific proposals of Year 2000, such as report card marks.

In May, new Premier Rita Johnston—who took the helm after Vander Zalm finally abandoned the sinking Socred ship—ordered a cabinet review of Year 2000.

In the summer of 1991, Hagen axed dual entry, leaving school boards to deal with the question of what to do with the 14,000 kids who began kindergarten in January: Should they continue in kindergarten or go to grade 1? The end of dual entry offered some vindication to the opponents of Year 2000 and some ammunition for them to say "I told you so." The proponents of the program, meanwhile, became both gun-shy and sceptical. They feared backlash from future attempts at reform and at the same time wondered whether their political masters would follow through with their grand promises. The death of dual entry fed doubts: nobody could be sure if Year 2000 was sacred anymore and many teachers in the higher grades simply didn't believe reform of any sort was going to happen in their programs.

"It was a tough call," says Wayne Desharnais. Many delegations came to the ministry and told it not to get rid of dual entry, while many school districts complained that they weren't set up for multiple entry points. "It was really difficult to implement in the system," he says.

In response to the death of dual entry, Tony Brummet resigned his seat. He knew that the media would come to him and ask for his opinion and he says he wasn't about to lie, but nor did he want to stab the government in the back. "The only decent thing to do was step down," says Brummet. To this day, he insists that dual entry could have worked and it was killed only because of attacks by certain groups of parents who had political clout and whose kids were born in November and December.

On September 6, just as the province's schools were heading back to class, days before the election would be called, Hagen took action on the results of the cabinet review. He announced that intermediate and graduation program implementation would be delayed a year—the first two years of intermediate would become mandatory in 1992-93, the third and fourth years in 1993-94, and the final three years in 1994-95, while the graduation program would be implemented in 1995-96. Until that time, teachers and trustees had been crying for more time to implement the programs, begging the government to slow down on the pace of its ambitious reforms. But rather than embrace Hagen's announcement of a delay with open arms, educators lashed out. Here's why: the tone of his announcement didn't focus on giving the system more time but rather on injecting standards and accountability and getting business involved in the school system. It seemed that with Tony Brummet gone, Social Credit was beginning to wonder about this Year 2000 animal. Perhaps without Brummet to persuade them of its value, cabinet ministers found the document a little left wing, thought it would make the education system far different from the days when they went to school. Coupled with the trashing of dual entry, it had the effect of creating uncertainty around the government's intentions.

Doubt was cast on Hagen's commitment to the philosophy of Year 2000 by the September announcement because he called for letter grades in the intermediate program, public reports of student performance in each school district compared to the province as a whole, and a Provincial Education Standards Board that would in his words "provide an ongoing focus on standards, accountability and excellence." Hagen's most controversial decision was to appoint mining magnate Edgar F. Kaiser Jr.—a key backer of Bill Vander Zalm's 1986 Socred leadership campaign—to head a so-called citizens' committee to look into education, the External Advisory Committee on Education Reform. Not only was this committee a slap in the face to the Education Advisory Council, but also to educators, who were excluded from the "external" committee. In addition, Kaiser's resume read like everything the NDP and BCTF would despise: chief executive officer of Kaiser Resources Inc., former chairman of the Bank of British Columbia, former assistant to both the U.S. president and secretary of the interior.

Predictably, Hagen's action drew critical response from his namesake across the floor, NDP education critic Anita Hagen, as well as BCTF president Ken Novakowski. But even the less partisan BCSTA president Donna Jones was livid: "On the eve of an election, to hear that a program we've been working on for so long is suddenly put on hold—I'm sorry, I try not to be political but that's what it looks like to me. And it's playing politics with thousands of children." [1]

Former deputy minister Sandy Peel remains to this day extremely critical of Hagen's actions in his short term as minister. Peel points out that he killed dual entry even though a ministry survey revealed overall that parents thought it was good. "He talked to a couple of school boards that didn't like it and he axed it. He axed it arbitrarily," says Peel, adding that he would have tried to talk Hagen out of it had he still been the deputy minister. In addition, he feels the offset advisory group under Kaiser said to EAC that it was no longer relevant. "Literally from that moment on, things started going downhill," says Peel. "I'm being very blunt and Stan won't like that, but in looking back over it, I can see the absolute seeds of it coming apart right there."

THE 1991 ELECTION

Many people feared the Socreds would abandon Year 2000 if they won the election. But that didn't happen, and Edgar Kaiser didn't get his chance to head an external advisory committee. Premier Rita Johnston called an election days after Hagen's announcement and on October 19, the once-mighty Social Credit dwindled to a rump of six seats. The New Democrats led by Mike Harcourt became the government and the Liberals under Gordon Wilson, the new official Opposition.

Education wasn't an issue in the election. In general, the NDP supported the principles of Year 2000, although it was critical of certain aspects of the program and its implementation. Assistant deputy minister Jack Fleming recalls, "We knew if the Socreds hadn't done something, education was going to be a major issue in the next election. I think most people felt that they had essentially defused it as an election issue. If you look at the NDP party policy that they went into that election with, it's 85, 90 percent congruent with what the [Socreds' Year 2000] program was all about. From the opposition's perspective, from the BCTF's, I think they were resentful in a sense that the government had lifted one of their major attacking points coming into the election."

In January 1990, the NDP had released five discussion papers about Year 2000 aimed at teachers, trustees, parents, business and working people. In them, the party stated what it liked about the proposals and its areas of concern. The major criticisms raised in the series of discussion papers included: Year 2000 emphasizes skills development and job training over education; it doesn't address the difficulty of implementing change; the implementation time line is too short; a "Big Brother" system of record-keeping to hold accountability over the heads of teachers; testing drives the curriculum;

blurring subject and discipline lines in secondary school is a problem; businesses aren't prepared to handle the mandatory work experience proposal. In summary, "The changes suggested in the Year 2000 paper are not what the public had in mind when the Sullivan Commission hearings were held! People want to know their children will be well-prepared in all subject areas to meet the information explosion, to understand the past and to become active and caring participants in the world. There is no such guarantee with Year 2000: the suggested changes break down learning into discrete, observable, computable parts that are not necessarily significant." [2]

Despite its flaws, the NDP endorsed the philosophy of Year 2000:

> The New Democratic Party applauds the emphasis on enabling learners in the Year 2000 document. The language used to describe the primary program embodies progressive thinking. In fact, many teachers are already doing what is proposed. For teachers who are not, the NDP has considerable sympathy. We think that a good deal of time, help and in-service preparation should be given teachers as they prepare for significant changes within their classrooms and schools. The notion of a student's continuous progress is also an idea whose time has come; in fact this way of organizing for instruction has been adopted by many elementary teachers. We also support the notions of co-operative learning, peer tutoring and curriculum themes. [3]

When the NDP won the election, a lot of educators celebrated. The party, which hadn't been in power since 1975, was seen as a friend of education. With its overall endorsement of Year 2000, the NDP was welcomed by the program's backers. "What we were talking about was ideologically more in line with their thinking," says Graham Hunter of the intermediate program team. "I was convinced and we all felt, 'Here's our window of opportunity. If we can't get it in now we never will and we've got at least four years to do it.'"

It seemed as if the stormy days of uncertainty and conflict with Social Credit were over. But the things that were to occur during the first two years of NDP rule would leave many people in a fog.

---

1. "B.C. delay of education reforms assailed," *Globe and Mail*, September 7, 1991.

2. "The New Democratic Party of B.C. talks to School Trustees about the Ministry of Education's Year 2000 blueprint for education." Unpublished document, December 1989.

3. Ibid.

[5]
PARALYSIS BY ANALYSIS:
October 1991 – August 1993

As expected, the former education critic for the NDP became the new education minister in government. Anita Hagen, a former secondary-school teacher and longtime school trustee from New Westminster, took the helm. People who reflect on her two years in office criticize her lack of action: "the big pause," Janet Mort calls it; "paralysis by analysis," says trustee Jackie Tegart.

Jack Fleming says to this day he remains puzzled about what happened once the NDP was elected. "Essentially, we went through about one year of being unable to do anything," says Fleming. "We assumed it would be a fairly quick transition between the two governments. As it turned out, it was a very long, agonizing year and a half or two years of relative inactivity at that level. It's a well-known and observable fact that Anita Hagen was dragging her feet." She wouldn't give her approval to further drafts of the intermediate and graduation programs and wasn't strongly committing the government to Year 2000. But she also wasn't saying the government would re-examine the Year 2000 in light of NDP policy, nor even vigorously articulating what the party's policy was.

Says Fleming, "We must have gone through six or eight major replanning attempts to try to redevelop a context for the Year 2000 program . . . trying to reaffirm the government's commitment to that educational direction in the very broadest sense, to get them to commit to that publicly, to tell people out in the field that yes, this thing was still a go, that they were still essentially committed to it although they reserve the right to review and change it and make amendments to it. Those statements simply did not come. So the whole question came up, 'Is the Year 2000 floundering? Is it still there? What's going on there?'"

When ministry staff attended Education Advisory Council meetings, they would not put Year 2000 on the agenda, and if it came up, they would waffle and talk about the government going through a reassessment period, says Fleming. "That wore thin after a while. It became pretty obvious to people that there was something deeper than that but no one could put their finger on it. Even when the minister came to the Education Advisory Council, she would tend to talk all around it but wouldn't come to grips directly with the question of whether we're going ahead with this program or aren't we?"

"She just seemed frozen," says Janet Mort. "It was like she just got paralyzed and she consulted and consulted and consulted and consulted and never made any decisions." Mort, Fleming, and Oscar Bedard (assistant deputy minister for evaluation) spent days writing reports on the ministry's strategy under the new government, sent them to Hagen, and received no reply. "We were almost immobilized for six months just because there were no decisions. We kept writing reports," says Mort. Meanwhile, "Teachers were out there in the province saying, 'Well, is it on or isn't it on? I don't want to do all this work for nothing.' So there was a lot of consternation."

Why did this waffling happen? Some people say Hagen simply couldn't make a decision. One trustee describes her as "a rowboat with one oar. She couldn't find a direction, stand up, or be firm. She was trying too hard to please all sides."

Hagen certainly did emphasize what she called "the three Cs"— collaboration, consultation, and co-operation. Unfortunately, say people in the system, the result was more like confusion, consternation, and chaos. Under her tenure, the members of the Education Advisory Council dug into their traditional opposing positions. "They were not in there as advisors, they were there to battle each other, not to solve problems but to argue for predetermined policies. Their goal was to lobby for their policies, whether they're good for learners or not," says Kamloops superintendent Tarry Grieve. As a result of this and Hagen's commitment to consensus, adds Grieve, the minister "felt herself in a morass of never being able to make a decision."

It's obvious that Hagen was getting mixed messages on Year 2000. The BCTF hadn't endorsed it beyond the primary program, members of her own cabinet weren't totally thrilled with it, critics continued to slam the program, and the fiscal climate showed that money was going to be tight, yet politically Year 2000 represented something that fell in line with NDP ideology and educationally it seemed like a good idea. The conflicting voices in her head must have been raucous.

There are other theories why she refused to embrace Year 2000 and stand up for it publicly. "Her agenda had essentially been lifted from her. She wasn't going to be able to be the revolutionary in the small-R sense," says Jack Fleming. "She really always felt that it was sort of Tony Brummet's program, it would never be her program. She couldn't see how to make it her program, to put her stamp on it. I think that bothered her to some degree."

Among the few who give any benefit of the doubt to Anita Hagen is Nancy Sheehan, UBC's dean of education: "Anita was in at a very, very difficult time," says Sheehan, adding that it's unfair to criticize Hagen as spineless. "There was nothing that the minister could have done to calm the public down."

Hagen had a lot on her plate in addition to education—she was also deputy premier and minister responsible for multiculturalism and human rights. "It swamped her," says Sandy Peel. "It darn near killed her."

Burnaby superintendent Elmer Froese says, "The loss of Anita Hagen as a minister of education is one of the real tragedies of all this. She was the victim of a series of things that were not of her own making. To her credit, she hung in there speaking for the Sullivan commission when she had virtually no support either in cabinet or from her own ministry. She inherited a badly flawed implementation process." He says Hagen was caught in the dilemma of choosing between "what the public saw as the right thing based on its perceptions and what was educationally the right thing."

To those who say she wasn't firm in making decisions about Year 2000, Hagen responds, "That's a perspective that I accept as being there. It's one that I struggled with as well. Within our ministry the move to be more effective in terms of our communications was one that we didn't handle as well as we might have and that was a constant challenge for me as well." But in her defence, she counters that she had a lot more to deal with than just education reform. "There were other issues that were taking considerable time and attention and public attention," says Hagen. "I sought to really develop a much broader [consultation] table where we could deal with the issues. That took time. It was compromised, too, by labour relations that were acrimonious and difficult."

Hagen said she started working on some of her concerns about Year 2000 as soon as she became minister. She wanted to make the reform process less centralized, shifting it more toward the school level, toward the people who would put the theory into practice. She also says she had reservations about the primary-intermediate-graduation program division, especially since the intermediate program's grade 4 to 10 structure didn't match the divisions of schools into elementary and secondary.

But she didn't survive long enough as minister to change the structure, as the next chapter reveals.

THE 1991–92 SCHOOL YEAR

After the election, the NDP government began cleaning house in various ministries. In education, the first to go was the man at the top, deputy minister Wayne Desharnais, in January 1992. He was replaced by a non-educator, Valerie Mitchell. She leapt to the position from previous jobs in finance and facilities policy and as a Treasury Board analyst. "It was an intense and interesting and challenging period of time," says Mitchell of her tenure. "In retrospect, I don't think I could have anticipated all the things that came up."

Meanwhile, despite the change in government and deputy minister and despite Hagen's lack of commitment, the program teams kept working on the second version of their documents. The second version of the graduation program was released as a "working paper." The intermediate team finished its re-draft (intending it to be the final version of the program) before Christmas 1991, but the ministry wouldn't release it until the following spring, and when it did, it was again labelled a draft. The reason: Hagen did not want to approve it as a final version of policy. Says a ministry official, "There was a lot of concern over the substance of that intermediate program document and I know from people I spoke to that the minister was not that happy with it, but agreed to issue the document as a draft."

"She wanted to pause and take a look at where things were and make sure the directions where things were heading were the right directions," says Valerie Mitchell. "The document itself was written in a way that was very inaccessible to the general public. If you had to summarize what was in the draft document in a thirty-second bite, it was a really difficult task."

For a cabinet minister whose job is to set policy and let staff carry it out, Hagen was extremely hands-on with the intermediate program, looking at drafts and sending them back with her handwriting and instructions on them. "I think she was just befuddled about it all," says an insider. "I don't think she was telling them to go in any direction, she just knew she didn't like it so she kept sending it back."

Hagen's response: "Rewrites were there not to deal with substance but to try to make the communication of that substance more effective."

In February 1992, with Mitchell's ascendancy to the deputy minister position, Janet Mort of the innovations branch went looking for a vote of confidence. Wayne Desharnais hadn't liked the role of the branch during his tenure, but Mitchell refused to answer Mort's concern that the branch would be disbanded. On March 1, Mort handed in her notice effective June 30. She says she saw the writing on the wall for the branch—and for Year 2000.

In May, Hagen issued a "ministerial statement" in an attempt to silence the criticisms that she wasn't taking a stance on Year 2000. It satisfied no one. In essence, it said the ministry would continue to develop the intermediate and graduation programs, but it was far from a ringing endorsement. "Over the next year we will collaboratively continue to develop the Intermediate Program and encourage its implementation through specific resource assistance to schools and districts," wrote Hagen. On the graduation program, she added, "Over the next two years, the program, including new graduation requirements, will be finalized and implementation dates established." Those were the strongest passages on the programs in her statement.

On June 11, Mitchell (who must have been acting under Hagen's orders) fired Jack Fleming, assistant deputy minister in charge of Year 2000 and a twenty-year veteran of the ministry. One observer who doesn't want to be named calls that decision "a disaster, one of the biggest mistakes they made" because Fleming was highly respected around the province. "The ministry lost credibility. They also lost their best advisor. This is a man who's been in government twenty years, he's seen every trend come and go, he knew the system, he knew government, he knew politics, he could find the solution in government to anything if he really wanted to. The ministry got credibility in the field because Jack was there, so when he was fired, it was considered about the dirtiest, low-lying piece of work anybody could have done."

Fleming had proposed to Mitchell a new organizational plan for his schools program branch to take in the tasks of the dying innovations branch. It was going to mean changes for some other senior bureaucrats. Sources say they didn't take kindly to the idea, they had Mitchell's ear, and she rejected his reorganization. Two weeks later, he had designed another version and took it to Mitchell the day he was fired.

"He was so excited," says a ministry staffer who was there. "He went down there saying, 'I think this one's really going to work. She's going to like this. I think this one could be really exciting.'" He disappeared into Mitchell's office for an hour and a half, then reappeared to call staff into a meeting in the boardroom. "He had been told to be out of the building by 10:30 and have his keys handed in. He was sent upstairs to call his staff together and tell them he'd been fired. And then he was to tell us to stay in the room and wait for Oscar [Bedard] and Valerie [Mitchell] to come and speak to us, it was Oscar who would be taking over Jack's job. He sat at the head of this table—this wonderful man who was so kind and so good to everybody and was the rock of Gibraltar for the staff in the ministry—he sat and cried at the head of the table, tears running down his face. He did it in the most dignified fashion, saying, 'Apparently I'm not going to be with you people any more.' People in the room were hugging each other, sobbing, tears running down faces, one woman was sobbing so loudly it was like screaming. It was just the most ungodly thing I'd ever seen."

Why was Jack Fleming fired? It's ironic, considering that it was the NDP who brought him into the ministry in 1972, hiring him as deputy minister during the party's previous stint in government. Some people say the BCTF wanted Fleming's head for something he did after the Socreds regained power: Fleming was responsible for axing the ministry's research branch, formed by the NDP to develop policy initiatives. The group included Ken Novakowski of the BCTF. Perhaps that attributes far too much power to the BCTF—despite the claims of some critics, it's shallow to assume that the union holds the NDP like a puppet on a string. Others point to the fact that Fleming was so closely associated with Year 2000 from day one and the government was having serious doubts about the program.

"He passionately believed what he was doing was critical to the lives of children," says an observer. "You know what passion does. He would go into senior bureaucrat meetings and he was very stubborn, very, very stubborn, and he wouldn't stop. When no decisions were being made, he pushed for a decision and when the wrong decision was being made, he said it was wrong and he said it loudly. I think that they thought they had a problem. Jack stayed with his passions and they weren't ready for passion, they'd had enough of passion. At that time they were kind of trying to slow the Year 2000 down and he was determined to keep it moving."

Fleming's take on the matter is, "If firing me would've stopped the program, and if that was what they wanted to do, they left it too long." Although he admits that he was concerned the government wouldn't commit to Year 2000, he says the genie was out of the bottle six months after the reform process started. "As long as there was a discussion going on around the essence of the programs, as long as that debate was occurring at that stage, that was all I cared about personally."

Fleming says his firing came right around the stage when it was time to "reel in" the teams and get them focused on producing final versions of their programs. The ministry was analysing responses from the field and was preparing to rewrite the Year 2000 framework and recast all three programs.

THE 1992- 93 SCHOOL YEAR

In the fall of 1992, policy director Jerry Mussio returned to the ministry from a secondment. By this time, the program teams and the remnants of the innovations branch had been brought under the school programs branch. Mussio's job was to end the confusion in the field over what Year 2000 was and get some clarity in the program documents.

"There was a lot of confusion about Year 2000 because people did not know really what it meant. In fact it had become a lightning rod for anything negative with the system," said Mussio. "All of the ills of the system were being put at the doorstep of Year 2000. I linked that to lack of clarity on the ministry's part about what it was they were trying to achieve in specific terms. I also observed that there was major confusion in many of the documents between how one goes about doing the business of teaching, the 'hows' of education (organizing schools, delivering services) with the 'whats' (what is it we're supposed to teach and kids are supposed to learn)."

To take Mussio's terms further, the prime role of the Education Ministry has always been to define the "whats" of education: establish a prescribed provincial curriculum, define the minimum hours of instruction, create the framework for accountability such as provincial exams, distribute funding to districts. The ministry had always kept its nose out of the "hows"—such issues as principles of learning and their implications for teaching methodology have always been delegated to the districts, the schools, and the teachers.

The ministry can help teachers upgrade their skills, says Mussio, but should not be mandating the hows of teaching. However, he found that the Year 2000 program documents implied that the ministry was telling staff that they must use certain techniques and elements—multi-age grouping, co-operative learning, themes. "There is no way that government can ever prescribe how people go about teaching," says Mussio. "What government can do is provide forums and vehicles for teachers to learn about new curriculum, to talk about teaching strategies, and so on"—in other words, professional development.

But rather than looking at education reform as a long-term process that would involve a certain amount of retraining by teachers, the program teams were attempting to change teachers' practice by issuing documents, by fiat: "Thou shalt teach this way."

The ministry's attempt to fix things in 1992–93 came through a behind-the-scenes working committee under Oscar Bedard, the new assistant deputy minister for education programs. Bedard came to the position with a lot of experience and connections in the field.

Hagen says the committee worked extremely well, the issues were addressed around the table, and recommendations came into the ministry. "We began to see considerable progress toward resolving some of the questions that were out there," she says. "Much of that work was completed by the time my term as minister ended." Hagen says the ministry realized that the program teams needed to be restructured to "have a more holistic approach" and says the ministry was moving strongly in that direction by spring 1993.

"There was a lot ready in the spring of '93," says Mitchell. But the problem then was that other issues—namely strikes—captured the ministry's and the public's attention. And after they were over, it was too late for Year 2000.

THE GROWTH OF OPPOSITION

Although there were bits and pieces of public opposition to Year 2000 during the previous four years, it appears from an analysis of the media coverage that the program didn't become a frequent target until 1993. Until then, there was the occasional critical newspaper column and letter to the editor, the odd complaint on phone-in radio shows, but no concerted, regular coverage of Year 2000 as controversial, with one exception. *B.C. Report* magazine had run critical stories on Year 2000 since the program was first proposed in the days of the Socreds. Once the NDP was elected, the frequency of the articles increased. A look at some headlines gives an idea of the tone: "Rebellion in the schools: A growing number of trustees and parents are fighting Victoria's Year 2000 plan"; "Learning to fight mediocrity"; "Why Johnny can't learn"; "Problem solving is not a priority;" "A dangerously fragile foundation"; "2000 ways to fail"; "A teacher describes why Year 2000 wouldn't work"; "Open rebellion against Year 2000." Where critical statements couldn't be made, the headlines posed doomsday questions: "Has competitive sport had it?" "Is it goodbye English lit?"

The story headed "Open rebellion . . . " (December 10, 1990) told of how two mothers pulled three children out of a school in the Arrow Lakes district because of Year 2000. This is open rebellion? The article also says Year 2000 "calls for all examinations, grades and marks to be eliminated." Another story in the magazine's news pages said, "When it is completely phased in, no children will fail and there will be no letter grades through grade 10" (September 7, 1992). And in an editorial, "Year 2000 is the catch-all phrase describing a radical and untested new curriculum that aims to protect students from such traditional educational touchstones as grades, marks, competition and distinct subject material" (June 22, 1992). *B.C. Report* has every right to its own political perspective, but what's not acceptable is factual errors.

The magazine also did little to make Year 2000 clear to its readers. Its June 1, 1992, issue included "Year 2000 Trackmeet Guidelines," which through word of mouth became accepted as reality by many. The magazine didn't clarify the satirical nature of the so-called guidelines: instead, it printed them as a sidebar to a news story and appended: "Note: Found on an elementary school bulletin board." The guidelines included: "High jump—There is no bar, as hitting it could produce an attitude of failure. Sprint—No set distance. Participants may run in any direction they wish, for as far as they wish. We feel this makes for a less stressful event. Long jump—In the spirit of non-competition, remember this: 'It is not how far you jump, but that you jumped.' The tape measure has no gradations." And so on, concluding with, "Awards—Everyone will receive a huge trophy with everyone's name on it. In these events, we have attempted to establish a non-competitive, no-failure situation. This is to better prepare our young people to be successful in our non-competitive society."

The fact errors and half-truths spread about the Year 2000 by *B.C. Report* weren't the only things the magazine did that helped to galvanize opposition to the program. The choice of coverage in its news pages smacked of a campaign against Year 2000. News stories focused on the pockets of opposition—a few upset parents in Fruitvale, a dump-2000 group in Vanderhoof, a former teacher taking her daughter out of the public system, a Fort Nelson trustee trying to start an anti-2000 network (and his fax number was included). In a province as big as B.C., it's easy to find some people opposed to as big an education reform as Year 2000. Translating this minimal backlash into a groundswell of public discontent was misleading.

B.C. Report's contribution to the anti-Year 2000 sentiment should not be underestimated. For the program's opponents, it became their medium of communication and the information printed in it became their weapons. No other single medium attacked Year 2000 as much.

Another critic of Year 2000 with a media platform was former teacher Andrew Nikiforuk, the Alberta-based education columnist for *The Globe and Mail.* He regularly referred to Year 2000 in his weekly column and regularly criticized it. He did not resort to outright lies about Year 2000, but let the rhetoric shine through. Calling Year 2000 "a grand and very authoritarian educational experiment with no field controls," Nikiforuk wrote, "I listened to beleaguered teachers and angry parents mostly condemn the program and one hapless ministry official, Jerry Mussio, perfunctorily defend what may well become the biggest fiasco in Canadian, if not North American, schooling."

Nikiforuk's most incisive criticisms were of say-nothing anecdotal report cards and the ministry's failure to impose yardsticks to measure the program's eventual success or failure. Other criticisms he borrowed from opponents (like the UBC Faculty of Arts report complaint that the emphasis on the learner denies the importance of teacher and family). And other criticisms pointed at problems with school bureaucracy, not Year 2000 pedagogy, or else were mere anecdotal evidence and comments from disgruntled parents.

"He did capture the concerns and feelings of a number of parents and a number of educators. At the same time what he did not do was a balanced presentation of the various elements of the Year 2000," says a ministry staffer who feels Nikiforuk's claims that Year 2000 included no standards, no grades, and no values were simply wrong.

Nikiforuk's personal perspective is best revealed in his book *School's Out.* Many of the points he raises are extremely valid: schools' primary responsibilities are to teach kids to read, write, and do math; throwing money at schools is no guarantee of quality; demands by business that schools produce skilled workers are a problem; private schools are not the solution; parents must stop treating schools as day-care centres. But Nikiforuk gives away his ideological perspective by blaming the failures of schools on "the overthrow of the school's original mission by sweet-sounding progressive dogma." The reasons behind the inadequacies of schools are far more complex.

Nikiforuk and B.C. Report were the two most visible critics of Year 2000. Other media coverage was more benign: articles in The Province and the Vancouver Sun generally gave both sides of the story, and critical columns in their pages seemed to be met with a relatively equal number of opinion pieces in favour of Year 2000. Occasionally certain writers slammed the program, sometimes repeating the myths.

"You would think after reading the paper that no kid would ever have to have an evaluation, that they would just go on from year to year in their merry way, doing what they wanted to do," says Valerie Overgaard of the Vancouver school district. "Even the Year 2000 — which was slightly extreme — never had those kinds of notions. The public outrage came from misconceptions."

But what was the Education Ministry doing to counteract the myths that were flying about Year 2000? Nothing, it seemed. Jim Sherrill of UBC calls it the "worst PR I've ever seen in my life. There was never any intention there would be no competition, but that was the public perception. The point was to move the emphasis away from competition. There's going to be competition whether you like it or not."

The reasons behind the bad public relations will be discussed next chapter.

It's important to note the broader political context of 1993 and its effect on perception of schools. The Charlottetown Accord constitutional referendum had recently failed, giving momentum to a backlash against the perceived elites of society. Support for the right-wing Reform party was growing as people bought into its emphasis on slashing the country's deficit. In general, people were politically grumpy, especially in British Columbia, which rejected the constitutional referendum by the biggest margin in the country and would soon send two dozen Reform MPs to Ottawa.

On the education front, the national grumpiness was revealed in February 1993 in a poll by Angus Reid for Southam News. It said 46 percent of Canadians—and 49 percent of British Columbians—

felt the quality of education was worse than it was twenty-five years ago. Thirty percent of respondents rated the system as better than twenty-five years ago. The poll revealed a drop in the public's esteem for education compared to 1986: when a similar poll was conducted, only 36 percent said the system was worse than twenty-five years earlier, compared to 42 percent who called it better.

Around this time, groups and self-proclaimed critics were springing up on the attack against the perceived failures of the education system: they included the Ontario-based Organization for Quality Education, under president Malkin Dare, a former teacher; Alberta radiologist and charter-school advocate Joe Freedman, and the group Albertans for Quality Education. These groups started to get mainstream media coverage and their rhetoric helped foster the attitudes expressed in polls like the one by Angus Reid.

This was the unfriendly political climate in which the Year 2000 reform was taking place. But even more important was the link created in the public's mind between the program and the perceived failures of schools. Even though Year 2000 wasn't implemented beyond grade 3, its reputation suffered because of the public's perception that the system wasn't responsive and wasn't producing good quality graduates. People who didn't like the school system saw Year 2000 as the cause. This is "educational jingoism," in the words of Kamloops school board chairman John O'Fee. "You can pound your fist on a table and criticize the hippy-dippy, airy-fairy stuff that goes on in schools and you're bound to get applause."

The contradiction in all of this is that people critical of the current education system were in effect demanding that schools stay with the status quo. North Vancouver superintendent Robin Brayne translates this into an axiom: "Public schooling never looks better to the public than on the eve of imminent change." U-Vic's Tom Fleming adds, "Public schooling *only* looks good to the public on the eve of imminent change."

Even Liberal leader Gordon Campbell acknowledges that some of the criticism of Year 2000 was misdirected. His party held an education forum soon after he became leader. "People came and they were just virulently opposed to the Year 2000 proposals. We asked the question, 'How many of you have actually read the Year 2000 program?' I'd say three people out of sixty put up their hands. A lot of frustration was building up through the whole system and the [Year 2000] label became the catch-all for people's concerns."

Year 2000 became symbolic of people's disgruntlement with education no matter what they were concerned about, says Arthur

Kratzmann of the Royal Commission. He recalls a meeting in the Okanagan at which a businessman complained that he was hiring high school graduates who couldn't spell, so he and others had formed a committee against Year 2000. Of course, Year 2000 was nowhere near the high schools and could in no way be blamed for a grade 12 graduate who couldn't spell. Kratzmann says only a "selective minority" was making noises about Year 2000, but they were loud.

How extensive was the opposition? The ministry received hundreds of letters of complaint, but did they represent the majority view among the parents of the province's 600,000 students? People weren't marching in the streets like with the so-called tax revolt of 1994. There were concerted bits of organized opposition: a Pouce Coupe truck driver named Don Coulter started a group called CARE—Concerned Adults for Responsible Education—which spread across the province and whose goal was the demise of Year 2000; the group Teachers for Excellence in Education—which opposes the right to strike and closed-shop schools—lobbied against what it called the "laissez-faire" nature of Year 2000.

The book *Class Warfare* sketches the links between the political right and the "grassroots" education lobby groups that have sprung up across the country. Although not all the critics of Year 2000 were political conservatives, links can be drawn between right-wing thought and a large number of Year 2000's opponents from the general public. Yet the people who backed Year 2000 in the system didn't see where the opposition was coming from and did little to debunk the myths being spread among parents. Supporters of the program "didn't assume we were in the midst of an ideological battle, they thought they had a challenge of implementation," says BCTF research director Larry Kuehn.

It's important, however, not to dismiss all the criticisms as ideologically driven, by any means. "It wasn't simply that [certain critics] were loud, there were just many opportunities for sloppy implementation of the Year 2000 and mindless implementation. There were enough examples of failure, enough illustrations of misapplication that it seemed like the whole thing was useless," says Roland Case of the intermediate steering committee.

Some of the things that angered the general public were changes that had little impact on how students are taught but which shattered people's perceptions of the way schools worked. The biggest one was changing the names of grades—rather than kindergarten to grade 3, the primary program would be called P1 to P4; in the intermediate program, grades 4 through 10 would become I1 to I7;

and grades 11 and 12 would shift to G1 and G2 to signify the graduation program. Utter silliness, considering that the rest of North America (except Quebec) speaks the language of kindergarten through grade 12. It made the public see the reform as strange and unfamiliar and therefore questionable.

Some teachers' interpretations of Year 2000 philosophy caused lots of problems. "We don't correct spelling anymore" was a common misunderstanding of the primary program's suggestions for teaching kids to read. One can imagine how justifiably angry parents could become upon hearing something so foolish.

Similarly, the theory of constructivism was misconstrued as being "kids do their own thing." Teachers were explaining the theory this way to parents, whose understanding became "Teachers can't teach kids anything." Naturally, that too made for an awful lot of irate parents.

The public also had legitimate axes to grind over certain teachers' attempts at writing anecdotal report cards. They interpreted the instruction to "describe what the child can do" as "don't say what the child needs to work on." The results were horrendous: report cards that made nonstatements such as "Alexander can choose a book at his own reading level and read successfully." [1] Either the ministry did not explain what a good anecdotal report card should be or else certain teachers didn't pay attention during that part of class. Even well-written anecdotal report cards bothered many parents because they lacked letter grades. That's because most every adult went through a school system that ranked kids from A to F: that which is familiar is most comfortable.

Robin Brayne blames the backlash on a lack of clarity in the Year 2000 programs. "The Year 2000 was like a giant philosophy of education that never really took flight because no one ever made anything concrete," says Brayne. "This whole reaction to standards, assessment, the fixation with report cards and letter grades all came as a consequence of the public truly believing that nothing was going to be taught because there was no focus."

The critics "were pointing out things that were known to us," says Jack Fleming. "In retrospect, we and the Royal Commission ought to have spent more time on the assessment and accountability issue. We didn't spend much time on that because everybody was focused on the other end, trying to actively change the focus of education to the learners." The questions of how programs would work and how teachers would do certain things had yet to be answered. "So it was an easy thing to attack, and in retrospect, I wish we had done more work about that."

Colleen Politano, a member of the primary program team, says the biggest mistake was not emphasizing that basic skills and accountability measures would be part of Year 2000. "We went out and we said to people with great evangelism, 'This is so wonderful, this is good for kids, this will make better lives for your kids, they'll have jobs.' And we were so enthusiastic and we weren't—in my opinion now—wise enough to say, 'Of course we'll have reading, of course we'll have writing, of course we'll have grammar, of course we want good spelling.'"

The ministry's slow reaction to the criticisms of Year 2000 was nearly fatal. But the final blow had nothing to do with the education reform but everything to do with the public's view of the school system: teacher strikes.

STRIKES

Labour disputes dominated the education news from February to June of 1993. In February, Quesnel teachers were on strike for three weeks, and in February and March, rotating strikes hit New Westminster and Surrey districts. Labour disputes came and went across Vancouver Island, the Powell River school board locked out its teachers in late March, and Maple Ridge teachers went on strike April 1. The issue really exploded in May when the two biggest districts in the province—Vancouver and Surrey—were shut down by strikes for three weeks, leaving 100,000 students at home a month before final exams.

The NDP cabinet was accused of dithering and took a lot of heat in the press for not intervening in the disputes. In late May, conflict of interest commissioner Ted Hughes declared that the several ministers whose spouses were teachers (including Premier Mike Harcourt) could participate in cabinet discussions of the strikes. The government promptly rushed in back-to-work legislation and binding arbitration to end the disputes, but not before considerable damage had been done, both to the government's popularity and the public's attitude toward the school system.

Anita Hagen says it became difficult to concentrate on Year 2000 during the strikes. "I remember the discussion: 'Shall we soldier on at this stage of the game?' and I said, 'Yes, we have to, but we know that we're not going to get people's attention and we won't have the focus while we're in the midst of labour disputes because schools are closed.'"

Hagen says her stint in office came at a complex time. "Everything that had to do with budgets, labour relations, all of that got mixed up in the business of the change agenda," she says. "We went through a period of reasonable stability but it was difficult in the second year once we started to be into major, major job action."

With strikes dominating the ministry's agenda in the first six months of 1993, little attention was paid to fixing the problems of Year 2000. And once June was over, little happened with the school system during its annual summer hibernation. It would face an abrupt wake-up call the following September.

---

1.   "Parents give Year 2000 a failing grade," *Vancouver Sun*, February 9, 1993.

[6]
WHAT WENT WRONG?

A senior education ministry official was visiting an uncle in 1993. "What's this Year 2000 crap?" asked the uncle, who's in his eighties. The official continues the story: "Here's my uncle, he's an immigrant, he's been retired for over twenty years. I asked him, 'Well what do you mean, what's your view of Year 2000?' And he says, 'Well they don't teach reading, there's no report cards, kids do their own thing, and my taxes are going up.' Then he turned to me and says, 'Well you tell me what Year 2000 is.' So I just blurted something out like, 'Well, it's about ensuring that all kids are able to read and write and do arithmetic and also doing a better job for those who don't want to go to university, who want to get a trade, and stuff like that.' And he said, 'Well why in the fuck doesn't the government say so?' That conversation, just sort of in a nutshell, I knew that we had a very serious problem."

The very serious problem that the Education Ministry had was communication. The immigrant uncle—who gleans his information from conversations with friends, the local paper, CKNW radio, and BCTV—was a good barometer of public opinion. How was it that someone came to think that Year 2000 meant "they don't teach reading, there's no report cards, kids do their own thing?" Since 1990, once Sandy Peel and Tony Brummet—the two major architects of Year 2000—were gone, telling the public about the program was a low priority. Rumour mills and *B.C. Report*—not the ministry—drove public opinion. Despite the complexity of the program and the difficulty for the public to envision it, the ministry did little to explain it. Even when the criticisms started to fly, the explanations lacked depth and specificity and couldn't counteract the bad reputation the program was getting.

"In the absence of communication from the government of exactly what was being done, those who were critical tended to have the field largely to themselves," says Ray Worley, former BCTF president.

To say that the death of Year 2000 is a result of bad communication is only part of the story: it's a symptom of what went wrong, but the root cause goes still deeper. The question to ask is: Why did communication break down? The answer is that the reformers did not know how to implement and, most importantly, foster change. That's what this chapter describes.

WHY COMMUNICATION IS IMPORTANT

"If you look at any set of literature around the concept of managing change, it requires exceptional communications," says Sandy Peel. "It requires that things be defined clearly and communicated well and followed up on." The questions that must be answered include: Why are things different? What's this going to accomplish? Why is this going to be better for students? How is it going to be delivered in the classroom? "You've got to sort of have an out-of-body experience," says Peel. "Put yourself in the place of a parent who rightly has all these questions in their mind. If you can't answer them, why should they buy it?"

The Year 2000 communication plan Peel conceived as deputy minister was left to fell apart. "The concept of working with the curriculum teams as these changes were coming along and preparing parent packages for the schools, making sure that people in the schools were briefed in terms of how to deliver them and what was going to happen, that all fell off the table."

The BCSTA complained to the ministry early in the process that communications were lacking and that the result was uncertainty amongst public and staff. Jackie Tegart, the former BCSTA president, feels the ministry didn't explain the genesis of Year 2000 in the Royal Commission, and as a result, people thought the program was imposed without public consultation. "There seems to be a lot of people who think that this stuff came out of the blue when really it was a comprehensive process," says Tegart. "The backlash on the implementation was predictable. If you don't start talking to the public and letting them know what you're doing and what you're doing well, there is going to be a backlash like you haven't seen before."

"A lot of the backlash was predicated on lack of knowledge," says the BCTF's Ken Novakowski. "If there's anything that can be said about the Year 2000 program and what happened is that it was a failure to communicate."

The job of public relations was in Janet Mort's hands and she says, in retrospect, the ministry should have done more work selling the program to the public rather than leaving the PR to schools. "We really missed the boat on the public and parents. We counted on school districts to sell to parents and they couldn't or they didn't," says Mort.

The innovations branch designed half-page newspaper ads proudly announcing the educational benefits for children entering the new primary program. They weren't approved. "I think [then-deputy minister Wayne Desharnais] was nervous about the amount of money that we would have to spend on it and nervous about being criticized for it," says Mort. "My instructions became, 'You can be high-profile with the school districts but keep it out of the public eye.'"

The ministry did some selling to the public, but not much, says former assistant deputy minister Jack Fleming. "We were trying to walk a fine line between taking any money from the programs and spending it on marketing and all that kind of attention-grabbing stuff. Public marketing, which is extremely expensive, wasn't easy to do. Most members of the cabinet were not able to stand up smoothly and talk about what we were trying to do."

Fleming says ministry staff knew they needed to communicate with parents but found they weren't easy to reach. "The best marketing devices we had were schools. We had to get schools committed to understanding why they needed to articulate [Year 2000] to the parent groups." He says a lot of effort went into communication for the primary program and the strategy worked well.

But the intermediate and graduation programs did not see the same effort and success. Former deputy minister Valerie Mitchell admits that the government failed to do a good job of communicating what was going to happen after the changes to the primary program. The message the government wanted to get across—why there was a need to change the higher grades and what the changes would be—was lost amid a host of other messages, sometimes con-flicting ones, she says.

Program Teams and Documents

The communication problem begins, like most stories, at the beginning, with the writing of the draft program documents. Royal Commis-sion report author Tom Fleming says the educators on the teams typically "ignored the public. They didn't pay attention to how it was going to play." The teams always thought of other educators as their audience and pitched their wares with their colleagues in mind. When you lose sight of the public, when you're only con-cerned with what the professionals want, education reform won't work, says Fleming.

But not only did the program teams forget the need to commu-nicate to the public, the communication to their colleagues was poor. Much of it was caused by the inability of the teams—particu-larly the intermediate team—to write clearly.

"There was this tremendous inability to get beyond the slogans," says Roland Case, who sat on the intermediate steering committee. "What was remarkable was when you finally put it in clearer lan-guage, people would say, 'Oh, I didn't know we agreed to that.' That's the seductive nature of slogans. Unless you get to that sec-ond level—what exactly do we mean—it disguises rampant and radical and often conflicting things."

Some people gave the team the benefit of the doubt and assumed that program policy needed to be vague and they waited for the docu-ments on curriculum and assessment. But when they came out, says Case, "They were atrocious. They were the most pathetic, mindless doc-uments issued. They were immediately thrown away as useless."

The teams' lack of clarity was felt all the way to the top. Anita Hagen says that when she read the documents, "It was hard for me to really get at the essence of the message. Often they were lengthy and the product of a committee rather than the product of some-body who was a communicator. What we were trying to do was make sure the final draft would be clearer, less lengthy, more cogent, more focused so that the intent would be clearer to a broader public." Hagen says the documents weren't written with the idea of communicat-ing to the public and the teams needed help in making them clearer.

Milt McClaren of SFU says he's somewhat sad about the fate of the intermediate document. "I think the intermediate program could have been salvaged had the ministry been willing to bring together in a sustained effort some curriculum specialists . . . in a room for five to ten days of hard work. I think they could have come up with a document that made the links, made the parallels, established some clearer frameworks."

Poor communication wasn't always the fault of the teams. Many teachers misunderstood the intent of Year 2000 programs, sometimes because the documents explained them poorly but also because teachers didn't read them carefully. For instance, even though documents said it was up to the teachers to decide when to integrate subjects, many teachers thought integration was mandatory. Kamloops superintendent Tarry Grieve recalls attending a workshop at which a teacher said, "Do you know what they're going to make us do? They're going to make us all teach everything through a theme." Adds Grieve, "It didn't say that. People were taking strong stands without having read the document." Anecdotal report cards that told parents nothing are another example of poor implementation of Year 2000 reforms: teachers did not understand what anecdotal report cards should look like, and the results were disastrous.

Such misinterpretations are typical of teachers' response to education reform: they pick up on certain manifestations of a movement and believe that's enough, says David Robitaille, senior researcher for the Royal Commission curriculum paper. A previous example was the so-called new math: teachers thought that teaching kids how to multiply in base seven meant they were "doing the new math."

Teachers didn't have a fundamental understanding of the program, the theory behind it, or the reasons for it, says Robitaille's fellow researcher Valerie Overgaard. As with past movements such as progressive education, teachers swallowed certain methods but didn't assimilate the philosophy into their psyche.

BCTF research director Larry Kuehn blames some of this on the ministry, which he says wasn't explicit about the developmental and constructivist base for the program. Instead of generating discussion about these theories of learning, the ministry assumed the theory was already accepted and understood by staff.

Former Kamloops trustee Paula McRae says the education system tends to take up notions without working through how to implement them. "It wasn't good planning. [Ministry officials] make announcements, put out balloons, and say, 'This is the direction.' When we ask for the map of how we get there, the map's not there. People get up in arms because they can't get the answers."

In short, poor communication was a major problem behind Year 2000. The flawed communication began with the program teams' inability to articulate the philosophy behind the reforms and to pass them on to the education community and the public. The next question to ask is: Why was this allowed to happen?

LACK OF LEADERSHIP

As noted earlier, Anita Hagen waffled in her commitment to Year 2000. More importantly, she and her senior ministry staff didn't take the actions necessary to clean up the program's problems in the developmental stage. When asked to look back and comment on what, given the chance, she would do differently, she replied, "Move more quickly on some of the changes."

But the root causes of the program's failure remain elusive. Why didn't Hagen commit to Year 2000 more strongly? Why didn't she act more quickly on the problems? Why in the end did her party call it a failure? On the surface, public opinion sounded the death knell for Year 2000, but the fatal blows also came from other quarters.

Money is a factor that was unexplored by the media. The Socreds had budgeted $1.4 billion over ten years to implement the recommendations of the Royal Commission, an average of $140 million per year, peaking at the time Hagen was minister. When I asked her if the cost of Year 2000 was too high, Hagen said, "I didn't see it as a major problem, no." But insiders say the NDP, desperate to project the image of sound fiscal management, was terrified of the price of the education reforms.

"The cost of doing this well was formidable," says Roland Case of the intermediate steering committee. To improve the education system in a meaningful way requires more than just issuing edicts about teaching styles—it means educating teachers, not through one-hour workshops but long-term professional development. That's not cheap, Case points out.

"They didn't have the money," says Janet Mort. "I saw the budget that the [Social Credit] government committed to when they passed the Royal Commission policies and it started disappearing immediately. The NDP didn't quite know what to do with it because they didn't have the money, yet socially and philosophically it's on the right agenda. I think they used the parental outcry around letter grades as a way to say, 'Shucks, we'll shift direction.'"

Adds BCTF vice-president Peter McCue, "What they were trying to do was introduce change at a rate and pace that demanded a lot of additional resources at a time when they were beginning a process of cutting back."

Meanwhile, Hagen was hurt by internal problems within her ministry. Her neophyte deputy minister Valerie Mitchell had no background in education, had never tried to run a big, complex, diverse organization like a school system, and was in over her head, say many observers. Ministry veteran Jack Fleming had been fired as assistant deputy minister in charge of Year 2000, which demoralized the staff below him and made the field doubt the government's commitment to the program. The innovations branch had been disbanded and its function was basically being ignored.

"There were far too many rapid changes in the Ministry of Education and they lost track of what their goal and objective was in all of this," says Sandy Peel. He says this big dismantling of ministry leadership was the main reason the communication plan fell apart. The remaining staff didn't have "the knowledge, the strength, or the commitment to follow through."

"To really understand what happened you need to understand the internal tensions," says one insider. Although there's no question that senior staff in the ministry were shaken by the change in government after sixteen straight years of Social Credit, some people say the internal problems began under the Socreds as far back as the early days of Year 2000.

Former Kamloops trustee Paula McRae says it was a shock to the ministry to be subjected to the openness and questioning and significant change that followed the Royal Commission. "It has been a traditional and controlling ministry," says McRae. "They've always kind of set their own course."

One ministry staffer says the "traditional bureaucratic structures" were disrupted by the arrival of groups of people from the outside—including Janet Mort and the teams—and the decision to make them report directly to the deputy minister and external steering committees, leaving the regular ministry branches on the sidelines. That, coupled with the change in ministers and deputy ministers, meant that close monitoring of the teams' work was lacking. "You had people who've been brought in from the school system to work on these new programs—very good, very creative—but the linkage between their work and government strategic policy and direction was starting to get very fragile," says the staffer. "People were going a bit further and were dealing with stuff that I thought was not necessarily part of the Royal Commission agenda."

Meanwhile, there were turf wars between the teams and the innovations branch on one side versus the curriculum and evaluation branches on the other. Money was taken from the established branches and shuffled off to innovation, creating resentment against Janet Mort. Some $300,000 was whisked out of the hands of the curriculum section working on the Learning for Living program, leaving that department devalued and demoralized, pushed to the side as the exciting Year 2000 ball rolled forward.

Intermediate team member Phil Foster stayed on in the Education Ministry after the team disbanded. That gave him a chance to hear the "other side" of the story—the ministry's side—and he says that the bureaucracy's desire to assert its authority is one of the reasons for the collapse of Year 2000. "We were outsiders thrust into the bureaucracy. The reason we were thrown in was to try to change the bureaucracy, but in fact what we did was push them aside. The tide came back and swamped the whole thing," says Foster. He says the ministry branches waged a "constant power struggle" against the teams. "We were sort of these irritants to the system," he adds. "The factions fought back and got back to their original power positions in the ministry."

Another set of internal tensions focused on Oscar Bedard, executive director of the program development division and a vehement supporter of Year 2000. "To understand Bedard's utter devotion to the Year 2000, one had to hear him speak about it," says a steering committee member. "Passionate almost to the point of having tears in his eyes. He became so involved with the project, so emotional about it, it was his baby."

Bedard was passed over for two key Year 2000 jobs. The first was running the innovations branch, given to Janet Mort. Then, in the summer of 1990, deputy minister Wayne Desharnais split the assistant deputy minister (school programs) position into two, creating one ADM for curriculum and another in charge of evaluation. Jack Fleming, who was school programs ADM got responsibility for curriculum, while Bedard took over evaluation, a messy portfolio that he didn't want. He would have preferred curriculum—putting him in charge of Year 2000.

When Fleming was fired in 1992 and Bedard was given his job, many people in the province—rightly or wrongly—blamed Bedard. "I think people quietly turned on Oscar," says an insider. "He lost respect because people just assumed he had something to do with it because then he inherited the kingdom. He hadn't been too quiet about his unhappiness about being out of the lights."

Roland Case says Bedard was indeed zealous in his support for Year 2000 but was always thoughtful and professional in his approach. "Oscar, for all of his flaws, said schools don't exist to give teachers jobs, they exist to help these kids learn and make a life and feel good about themselves. That was the kernel, retooling our schools to teach kids in a way that will help them succeed."

Bedard, who is soon to retire from the ministry (where he is currently in charge of the field services division) did not consent to an interview for this book.

OPPOSITION AMONG TEACHERS

A major factor in the downfall of Year 2000 was opposition to the program by teachers. Although teachers were responsible for developing the programs and many of them hailed Year 2000 as a great way to help kids learn, there were plenty of teachers in the ranks who did not like what they saw coming. Their resistance compounded the flaws in communication and implementation.

Sandy Peel says certain teachers didn't want to understand the principles behind Year 2000. "You have a lot of teachers out there that don't want to see this change occur because it upsets them—and I think that's the fundamental motivation, not because it wasn't good for education. They were communicating with the parents. They were using the best tactic they possibly had: 'This isn't going to work for Johnny. We don't know how to do this.' If you're a parent and you don't know a damn thing about education, who are you going to believe?"

Year 2000 was asking teachers to shift their teaching style away from the classical lecture toward more interaction with students: teaching students rather than teaching subjects. Many teachers—especially veterans—felt there was no reason for them to change.

Peel says they felt that way because they were comfortable with their accustomed techniques. He says Year 2000 didn't upset good teachers but caused problems for "Mr. Brown and Miss Jones that have been teaching for twenty-seven years and have their yellowed lesson plans all written up. All of a sudden they're told you don't walk in on day one and lecture and write on the blackboard and make people learn formulas and do all that sort of thing. It was very frightening to a large number of teachers in the system."

Most resistance to Year 2000 came among teachers in the higher grades. For many secondary-school teachers, their disciplines are a big part of their professional identity. Think of it this way: a typical elementary-school teacher says, "I teach grade 4," while a typical secondary-school teacher says, "I teach English." A lot of secondary-school teachers saw Year 2000, with its emphasis on integration, as an erosion of their traditional role as subject specialists and perhaps the precursor to the disappearance of traditional academic disciplines.

Asked why certain teachers didn't like the Year 2000 graduation program, team leader Dave Watkins says, "It was different. It required change. It seemed to be putting more demands on them. It was questioning their world, if you like, threatening their world, maybe." He says the team was met with hostility by many teachers. "Even though we viewed ourselves as being fellow teachers, fellow administrators, they perceived us as being from the government. They didn't have many opportunities to vent their frustrations at someone from the government and here was a great opportunity."

Even those secondary teachers who supported Year 2000 were trapped by one of the system's fundamental contradictions: how to personalize learning and still prepare students for government exams. Although Year 2000 ostensibly said memorizing finite bits of knowledge isn't the purpose of school, the provincial exams at the end of grade 12 sent a completely different message to teachers and, perhaps most important, to the students.

All of this meant that there was anything but unanimity about Year 2000 among the province's 40,000 teachers. In turn, that left the leadership of their union, the B.C. Teachers' Federation, in a bit of a quandary.

THE BCTF's ROLE

No discussion of education in B.C. is complete without considering the role of the influential teachers' union. On the surface, the B.C. Teachers' Federation should have embraced the philosophy behind Year 2000 like a long-lost relative finally come home. The BCTF's political ideology is firmly rooted in the tenets of social democracy. The federation has taken stands against racial discrimination and nuclear submarines and spoken up for affirmative action and native land-claim settlements. According to a statement adopted by the federation in 1974, the purpose of education is "to foster the growth and development of every individual, to the end that he/she will become a self-reliant, self-disciplined, participating member with a sense of social responsibility within a democratic society."

Given this political philosophy, one would expect the BCTF to speak up for Year 2000, a student-centred program designed to meet the needs of more kids than just those who go on to university. But the BCTF's resolutions and policies belie that assumption, as do statements in the press during the days of education reform. BCTF officials did not endorse the philosophy behind Year 2000 and regularly condemned the way the program was being implemented.

If you ask BCTF leaders why they didn't endorse Year 2000, they'll tell you they faced the problem of a divided house. They say many teachers supported Year 2000, many others didn't, so the federation couldn't reach consensus. The contradiction in all of this is that the BCTF has taken positions on all sorts of substantive issues that weren't directly related to education—issues on which consensus must have been difficult—yet it didn't take a position on the principles behind the biggest education reform in the history of the province.

There's no question that a significant number of teachers opposed the reforms, but in fact, the federation's own research shows overall support for the program's pedagogy. The results of a random survey of teachers conducted in May and June of 1993 were published in the federation's newsletter the following October, a month after the government pulled the plug on Year 2000. On a list of seventeen items related to the curriculum, instruction methods, school environment, and assessment and reporting, teachers reported that they would prefer to use practices espoused by Year 2000 over the so-called "traditional" practices in all but one case—multi-age grouping. Teachers preferred child-centred instruction to teacher-centred instruction, focus on process over focus on content, integration over discrete disciplines, continuous progress over prescribed scope and sequence, and so on. Even when the results from secondary teachers were examined separately, the preferences fell on the Year 2000 side of the spectrum except for multi-age grouping and a slight preference for letter grades over anecdotal reporting. "Teachers would like to change teaching practice but are held back by restraints in the system," wrote BCTF research director Larry Kuehn in the October 1993 issue of *Teacher*. "The teachers' overall ideals for practice substantially supported the approaches identified with the Year 2000 program. Actual practice, however—both by the individual teacher and in the school as a whole—reflects more traditional approaches."

Observers say the reasons behind the federation's lack of support for Year 2000 run deeper than a lack of consensus about its pedagogy: it's all about politics.

"They're culpable for what happened," says Maurice Gibbons, SFU professor emeritus of education. "I can't understand why they turned around and crapped on it. Their resistance became the biggest hurdle." Gibbons says it seemed as if it was more important to the BCTF to oppose whatever the government did than support a forward-looking education reform.

Fellow SFU professor Marv Wideen is less surprised about the BCTF's unwillingness to support Year 2000. Wideen says the federation is "part of the conservative structure" in the education system, politically minded and far from educationally radical. "I don't think the BCTF [officials] know enough about education to really recognize what they had here. I would not hold them up as educational leaders in any sense of the word." He says (albeit facetiously) that former BCTF president Ken Novakowski wakes up in the morning and counts how many copy inches the BCTF received in the *Vancouver Sun* and *The Province*. "He doesn't wake up in the morning and read John Dewey." Adds Wideen, "If you begin to see everything in political terms, then substantive educational issues just become political tools. If they support your political ends, you'll support them. If they don't, you won't."

The BCTF was too busy with other political agendas to fight for Year 2000, says Richard Williams, the trustee representative on the graduation program steering committee. But once the NDP did its about-face on Year 2000, the federation was confronted with different education reforms that it definitely did not appreciate. "Now they're beginning to realize they should have spent a little more of their energy on Year 2000," says Williams.

BCTF research director Larry Kuehn, who doesn't like the direction the government has taken post-Year 2000, admits the federation could have worked harder to promote the program's philosophy. "It's something I regret, that we didn't take the evidence for a constructivist approach and go out and at least hold discussions about it. When the political attacks came we were in even more of a dilemma in taking a strong stand."

Asked if he wishes in retrospect that the federation had thrown more support behind Year 2000, Ken Novakowski replies, "That's an interesting question. The ground shifted and changed to a different set of principles from the government and I would have some regrets about that shift having taken place." He says the emphasis has moved away from focusing on learners toward responding to the business community's and media's perceptions of what's wrong with the school system. "It's been much more difficult for us to put forward the argument that [education reform] has to be good before we go ahead with it because the other countering argument is, 'This is what the public wants.' So whether it's good or not for the kid or whether it really improves their educational climate is not the issue. The issue is, 'Are we doing what the public wants?'"

So why wasn't the federation more positive about Year 2000? "We always are cautious, I guess, when it comes to things that affect the entire system," says Novakowski. He says the federation has always had an internal debate about whether it should struggle through the lack of consensus and take positions on pedagogical issues. "In some respects I would say, 'Yes, I think we should.' Maybe we should be showing that kind of leadership and vision in spite of the fact that we may not have consensus."

The BCTF executive developed its policies on Year 2000 through consultation with its representatives on the program steering committees, its professional development advisory committee, its council of provincial specialist associations (PSAs), and the PSAs themselves. "If it's been tested, piloted, proven to be effective and the resources are there to implement it, then we would go along with it," says Novakowski. "On issues when there wasn't consensus, we didn't take votes and say, 'Majority rules.' We tried as much as we could to reflect the voice of teachers and also to present what we felt were the processes that should be followed to make those kind of changes."

He adds, "It became very difficult when I was president to try and deal with a lot of these issues not on the basis of what I thought, because I wasn't elected on the basis of what I thought about social studies and all the rest of it. I had to try and reflect what came out of the groups that we had set up to look at these issues. What I favour, what I think should happen, isn't necessarily what the organization thinks should happen."

It would not have been reflective of the membership to support Year 2000, says vice-president Peter McCue, designated by president Alice McQuade to be interviewed for this book. "People who really wanted to push it ahead felt that we as an organization should have been saying, 'Yeah, go ahead, go ahead,' but we had an equal number of our members who were taking a totally different view of that."

"We were accused by teachers of dragging our feet and opposing the Year 2000 and not being sufficiently on board and we were criticized by other teachers of having leapt on the bandwagon of the Year 2000 and being enthusiastic supporters," says Ray Worley, BCTF president from 1992 to 1994.

Year 2000 was not even an issue between the two political slates within the BCTF—Viewpoint and TUFF (Teachers United for the Federation)—which differ in their support for "hard-line" trade unionism. "Everybody who was active in the organization realized the difficulty of taking a strong position one way or the other," says Novakowski. The political officers in the federation are "very sensitive to what members might think about any particular issue."

Rather than take a stand on the substance of Year 2000, the BCTF's statements were always about implementation, the principles the federation felt should be followed in bringing about change. In other words, they focused on the process of reform, not the content. The result was a tone that showed anything but support for Year 2000: the federation appeared to be one of the program's opponents.

"When the Year 2000 came out we never said, 'Way to go, right on, we're behind this,'" says Novakowski. "We tended to respond on process on a lot of it." He admits that the federation's position on the Year 2000 may have seemed ambiguous.

"We have never taken a position that the ideal secondary school would have [certain] changes," he continues. "The positions we've taken have been related to process, saying, 'In making changes we want to make sure it benefits the kids, the resources are there, they're manageable,' those kinds of things."

BCTF positions spoke less on the principles of education reform and "more on the implementation, the pace of the implementation, and the lack of involvement or the nature of involvement of teachers," says Peter McCue. "One of our immediate reactions was 'Too much too fast.' That's not an uncommon reaction for those of us who work in the system. Whereas we always believe in and support change to improve the system, we're also hesitant and leery about changes that are being made that are unproven and untested. The best change is change that emanates out of the practice of teaching. Throughout all our experience in our careers, we've seen many kinds of trends and developments that have come and gone. They're trendy for a short time and then they disappear.

"We tend to say, 'If any changes are going to be made, let's pilot them, let's test them, let's make sure that they are going to improve the learning situation of the kids that we teach,' rather than, 'Looks good, let's go with it.' Sometimes it's very frustrating that we take that approach for those people who want to make the change, be they politicians or education administrators or whoever they are. They become convinced that these changes are the right thing to do whether there's the pedagogical evidence for it or not and then we appear to be a stumbling block."

"Wherever we had the belief and the conviction that this was going to be something that worked, we did come out strongly," adds Novakowski. "The primary program: we were up front about it, we did everything we could, we made proposals to the ministry about how to help with the implementation and everything else. We were part of all that, very successfully I think."

The primary program was the only facet of Year 2000 that the BCTF supported in principle. The primary teachers' PSA endorsed the primary program, and as a result, so did the federation. "There tended to be a consensus among primary teachers," says McCue. Such was not the case with the intermediate and graduation programs. "Those were being imposed. Those did not arise out of the practice," he says. "Because it hadn't arisen from practice, there wasn't a cohesion around it, we did not take a position of pushing it because that would've been pushing it in the face of many people who did not feel that it was effective, good classroom practice."

McCue admits that the tendency to organize secondary schools around subject areas made for natural resistance among those teachers. But he adds, "If you can demonstrate anything to them that was successful in improving the learning situation for kids, they would only too willingly do what was necessary to make that happen in their classrooms."

Had there been more time and money for professional development, says McCue, perhaps more teachers would have seen the advantages to the programs.

Novakowski says the Year 2000 plan called for "major changes in the system but we didn't see what we thought was the comparable package of resources that would need to go with it to successfully implement it. We thought it was in some respects almost an idealistic view of how change could happen. We did not at any point feel that the issue of resources was being treated as seriously as the proposed changes warranted. Yes, there were resources but we always thought they were almost token in respect to the magnitude of the changes that were going ahead.

"We never enjoyed the full confidence of the Ministry of Education in our working relationship," continues Novakowski. "I don't think they ever really fully grasped the nature of what we were trying to say. I think they suspected that we were sort of trying to set up roadblocks. Whereas my take on what happened is we were very enthusiastic about the idea of changes, that we were positive about the general thrust of the Royal Commission, but we weren't interested in being party to a fiasco."

However, confidence and suspicion are opposing lanes on a two-way street. "I was getting reasonably good support from most of the partner groups but the BCTF was very suspicious and I'm not sure they ever did lose that suspicion about the process," according to the ministry's Jack Fleming. "It was partly a total lack of trust. There was the hope that the Socreds were going to get defeated in the next election. The BCTF was very interested in that, they weren't interested in helping the government find the way out of whatever dilemmas they saw them in. So for political reasons, I think they were not motivated to get on board and call this a glowing success. They felt that in fact some of the motivation of the government in [introducing Year 2000] was to put the BCTF on the spot and force them to either accept the educational agenda or resist it and look anti-progressive. I think the government did in a sense put them on the spot."

Milt McClaren of SFU tells of a meeting he had with senior BCTF officials just before the 1991 election. "I said, 'I've been involved in federation stuff for a long time. I've seen a lot of the statements you've made about learning and kids and what you believe in and it seems to me that these documents are far closer to your statements than any other documents you've ever seen and I don't know why you're not supporting this.' I didn't get an answer. There was just sort of embarrassed silence, foot-shuffling, and throat-clearing. It became evident to me at that meeting that it was a political decision."

"What we were proposing was very much something they could have agreed with in different times," says intermediate team member Phil Foster. "They said, 'But we can't possibly support anything that the Socreds are coming out with even though it sort of sounds like what we might want to support.' That's the trap we were caught in."

Another intermediate team member, Graham Hunter, says the team had an excellent relationship with members of the BCTF's professional development wing, but those federation staff members had no influence over the union's political wing. "They were so caught up in the political wars, they weren't looking at the educational aspects and that's the nature of the federation, unfortunately," says Hunter.

An interesting irony—and a little-known fact among the public—is that the BCTF benefitted from Year 2000. The federation was hired by the ministry to run "development sites," a kind of pilot project in which teachers and schools across the province tried out some techniques and structures recommended by Year 2000. The money that came in boosted the federation's budget. The government's public accounts show that in the fiscal years of 1992-93 and 1993-94, the BCTF received a total of $2,039,000 in grants from the Education Ministry. Compare that to the three previous fiscal years: a total of $691,000 in ministry grants to the federation.

All of the BCTF leaders' explanations that they didn't back Year 2000 because of a lack of consensus fail to get at the heart of the matter: politics. Regardless of its educational soundness or its political leanings, Year 2000 came from the wrong party for the BCTF.

Ken Novakowski denies that the federation's stance on Year 2000 had anything to do with political partisanship. "The organization takes a position that they think is in the interest of their members or of the public education system regardless of the government that's in power," he says.

The Social Credit architect of Year 2000, Tony Brummet, tells the following story: "I said to Ken Novakowski, 'Why can't we work together and take this as far as we can? Teachers want it.' And he said to me, 'You're the politician. You should know why I can't support anything that comes from your government.' I took a lot of umbrage at that."

Talk of the "flexibility" inherent in Year 2000 set off alarm bells: flexibility is a term that contradicts the idea of a contract, with fixed terms. Even though Year 2000 could have devolved more authority to teachers, contract language created inflexibility.

The timing of the changes was unfortunate, says former Kamloops trustee Paula McRae. The BCTF was in its first few years of full collective bargaining, immediately after Social Credit's attempt to weaken its power. Everyone, including administration, was on guard. "You couldn't discuss change without thinking of its impact on the collective agreement. If we could have got beyond that, we would have been closer to what we wanted," says McRae. "When they feel more secure, they'll be prepared to talk more openly about flexibility."

THE UNIVERSITIES' ROLE

The province's three universities also became formidable opponents for Year 2000. Although they had seats on the intermediate and graduation program steering committees, the universities felt left out of the process of developing Year 2000. University officials say that rather than being asked for their advice and expertise, they were made to feel like the enemy during strategy meetings on the graduation program. Not getting the post-secondary community onside was a big mistake.

The Education Ministry found out that it doesn't help its cause to spurn universities. The Faculties of Arts and Science at UBC criticized Year 2000 and the graduation program, as described in Chapter 4. Calling Year 2000 "a radically different vision," predicting that its effect would be to "undermine rigorous learning and discourage high levels of achievement," and arguing that assessment practice would "not provide reliable reports of the performance potential and abilities of university bound students" had no small effect. [1]

The universities carried a lot of weight and were especially able to get political attention during the ministerial tenure of Stan Hagen—a former advanced education minister. In fact, the number one recommendation in the UBC Faculty of Arts critique (issued in November 1990) said the faculty should "open new and more effective channels of communication [to the Education Ministry] in order to influence educational reform."

Critics of the universities say their motives weren't pure. The ministry's Jack Fleming says universities want the school system to be a big sorting mechanism, separating kids into those who fit the academic mould and those who don't.

"The threat for the universities was that we would no longer identify the top kids academically for them and provide them with statistics to make it easy for admission," says Fleming. "That was really the basis for their major concern though they phrased it in all kinds of other ways." He says they "brushed aside as anti-intellectual" the fact that 70 percent of kids don't go to university and schools must respond to their needs.

University administrators "wouldn't sit down and look at how this was going to work," says Sandy Peel. He acknowledges the need to limit university admission but argues, "Let it be on a person's ability to deal with issues and problems as opposed to some arbitrary scoring system that means very, very little in terms of what a person can do."

MISUNDERSTANDING CHANGE

In summary, these were the factors and the context affecting the Year 2000 education reform process: the documents explaining the reforms were murky; efforts at telling parents and teachers the reasons behind the reforms were lacking; teachers and the public misunderstood not just the theory of the reforms, but their substance; the political and bureaucratic leadership of the day offered only lukewarm support of the reform process and took little action to correct its flaws; the government didn't like the looks of the program's cost; major internal changes had disrupted and demoralized the Education Ministry; teachers, their union, and the university community resisted the changes. Meanwhile, teacher strikes were closing schools, media coverage about the reform process wasn't positive;

the political climate of the country emphasized fiscal restraint over social programs; and the electorate was just plain grumpy and mistrustful of political leaders.

Could any sort of education reform survive?

The obvious answer would be no, but that lets the backers of Year 2000 off the hook, as if the program's failure wasn't their fault in any way. There's no question that external factors made for stormy weather for education reformers, but had the boat been built properly in the first place, it would not have sunk. I trace the root of Year 2000's problems to a more basic cause than even the lack of clarity of the program documents: throughout the process, after the departure of Tony Brummet and Sandy Peel, the people at the helm did not understand *how* to change a huge system like education.

The Education Ministry seemed to think education reform by edict would work—issue some documents, tell teachers to do certain things, and that would be enough to get people to change. Such dictates work if you're asking staff to change a bureaucratic procedure: for instance, schools shall issue four report cards per year, in November, January, April, and June. But the kinds of changes in the Year 2000 program involved substantial changes to the professional practices of teachers, the organization of schools, the mind-set of people in the system. You cannot change attitudes and beliefs and their resultant behaviours by fiat. It requires long-term professional development. To follow the dichotomy preached by creative writing teachers everywhere, "Show me, don't tell me." Reform won't come about by *telling* teachers what to do, by ordering them to follow certain principles, but by *showing* them the reasons for the changes, their benefits, their effect on students' learning. Ultimately, staff will incorporate those principles into their daily practices, schools will incorporate them into their structure, and change will have occurred.

Two educators who offer the most compelling arguments on why school reforms usually don't work are Seymour Sarason and Michael Fullan. Sarason argues that most attempts at education change fail because they do not change what he calls the culture of the school. Fullan, dean of education at the University of Toronto, takes Sarason further and argues that changes also fail because they don't have an impact on the profession of teaching.

In his book *The Predictable Failure of Education Reform*, Sarason points out the inherent flaws of attempts at reform-by-fiat, such as Year 2000. "In the education arena, those who advocate such changes, especially mandated changes, are either ignorant of the predictable problems or so unsophisticated about the dynamics of institutional change that one can safely predict they will end up blaming the victims." He says those who mandate change fail to answer obvious and important questions: "What are the predictable problems? How embedded are they in the history, tradition, and organization of school systems? What courses of preventive action might be employed, at least to minimize these problems? When and why should we expect which outcomes?" [2]

Sarason writes, "Educational reformers have trouble understanding that change by legislative fiat or policy pronouncements from on high is only the first and the easiest step in the change process. . . . Content to remain on that first step, assuming as they do that the goals of change can be achieved by a process that could be called human mechanical engineering, insensitive as they are to what the change will activate in the phenomenology of individuals and their institutional relationships, they confuse a change in policy with a change in practice." [3]

Sarason specifically mentions what's involved in getting teachers to embrace the techniques of small-group or co-operative learning: "Implementing the method requires the unlearning of conventional attitudes, practices and assumptions and the learning of new ones, a difficult task for anyone. It requires literally a re-education." [4]

This is where Year 2000 backers fell short: they did not see the need to embark on long-term "re-education" (or, in words that sound less like Big Brother, professional development) of teachers. Sarason says schools have never assigned any importance to the intellectual, professional, and career needs of teachers. He blames this for a decline in morale among teachers after their first year, the tendency to slip into dull routine in their teaching practice, and the lack of success in attempts to improve schools.

To make the improvement of the quality of teaching "a norm, not a war" requires a change in the "organizational culture" of schools, says Sarason. The key is a change in power relationships to give teachers more power. The necessary result will also be a change in the structure and atmosphere of the traditional classroom, giving more power to students. [5]

In his book *The New Meaning of Educational Change*, Michael Fullan emphasizes the complexity of school improvement: it's not something that lends itself to simplistic solutions, nor can it be narrowed down to a single factor. He sketches six themes in implementing change successfully: build a collective vision of the change; plan for evolutionary change; share power; monitor the process to cope with problems that arise; restructure the power relationships in schools; ensure concrete professional development and support throughout the process.

These last two themes deserve special attention. Fullan emphasizes the need for power in the hands of individuals within the school system. "As individuals we cannot wait for or take as sufficient the actions or policy decisions of others," he writes, urging staff to create "an ethos of innovation," which, by bringing about change from within, preempts the imposition of change from outside. But change within individuals is impossible without restructuring the institution of the school, he says, in an argument similar to Sarason's call for changing the culture of the school. "The current school organization is an anachronism," writes Fullan. "It was designed for an earlier period for conditions that no longer hold." [6]

Education reform is only successful if it impacts the professional practice of teaching, says Fullan. In calling for continuous professional development, he asks for more than mere one-shot workshops. To bring about improvements in teachers' professional practice, training must account for the realities of the school system, address individual needs and concerns, and include follow-up.

The bottom line for Fullan, as the title of his book implies, is that people who want to bring about change must take into account the subjective *meaning* of the change to those who will be affected by it. If a reform means for a particular teacher that his or her teaching practices must change, the reformers must create the conditions that allow the teacher to adapt to the new circumstances.

Fullan and Sarason's theories apply to Year 2000. The ministry did not understand what it takes for people and for a system to change. Rather than look toward long-term professional development to change the practice of teachers, the ministry chose to issue documents telling teachers what to do. The most concise summary of the fatal flaw comes from UBC education professor Jim Sherrill, a member of the graduation program steering committee: "They were trying to change the system and not the teachers."

Former deputy minister Wayne Desharnais admits that the ministry's biggest error was changing curriculum rather than changing people. He says ministry staff were married to the long-held notion in education that changing program documents would bring about a change in the classrooms. "The focus should be on people," says Desharnais. "If you're going to change anything, you've got to spend a lot of time working with people, making them comfortable with the change, giving them the skills and abilities to allow them to change. If the people don't make it work in classrooms, it's not going to work."

So why wasn't this done when he was deputy minister? "To be blatantly honest, the notion of spending a lot of money on teachers was not very acceptable to the government of the day," says Desharnais. "There was not a lot of support for pouring a lot of money into teacher professional development."

He says the Education Ministry and the current government are still making the same mistakes. "They're continuing to try to set out in stone all the elements and pieces and nuances of an intermediate program or a graduation program and it's not going to work," says Desharnais. "Trying to write that into a document is a no-win situation."

"This is a tough system to move ahead," says North Vancouver superintendent Robin Brayne. "There's a lot of inertia in a system that teaches some 200 programs in 2,000 locations to 600,000 kids with 40,000 employees. That's a big battleship to turn and it was tough to turn on just rhetoric."

Efforts at improving schools always face problems. Along the way, the reforms need fine-tuning, there are tensions between the different goals for schools, there are bound to be hitches and controversies and opponents. The people who want the system to change must manage those predictable resistant forces—they should not come as a surprise, leaving the leaders floundering about what to do. Leaders must be prepared to answer the natural questions and to support staff when problems arise. But the people engaged in Year 2000 did not have a good enough handle on the bureaucratic complexities of accomplishing everything that needed to be done on such a large scale.

"The trick of getting a system to change is to get the people involved to feel that they have a stake in it, some commitment to it, not just pouring it or laying it on them. Everyone knows that's the wrong way to do it," says David Robitaille of UBC.

His colleague Charles Ungerleider adds, "What no one had figured out is if you're going to bring about change in anything, ensure the involvement of the people involved in the change."

Or as former Sooke trustee Richard Williams puts it, "You can top-down all the changes you want, but unless the teachers feel part of those changes, they aren't going to happen."

This is not to support the argument put forward by Year 2000 opponents that they weren't "consulted" about the change. First, the Royal Commission listened to the views of the province; then the Education Ministry checked with lobby groups before acting on the commission recommendations; then more than 26,000 people responded in writing to the Year 2000 draft framework document (more than the number of submissions to the Royal Commission); and then feedback was solicited on each draft program document—the intermediate program alone prompted more than 3,500 written responses. The problem came after consultation—during implementation. During that process, staff didn't feel they had ownership or a stake in the program because professional development was minimal.

"It's quite a hopeless situation if we think we're going to leave the improvement of schools to policy-makers. It'll just get worse and worse and worse," says SFU education professor Marv Wideen. "We have learned over and over and over again that politicians cannot improve schools, curriculum-makers cannot improve schools, academics like me cannot improve schools, but what we can do is support the efforts of teachers to improve schools. That's not what's coming down with these mandates."

Wideen supports the principles of Year 2000 but says the Education Ministry went about implementing the program the wrong way because schools can't be improved from the outside. "What you're assuming is that some bureaucrat sitting in Victoria who hasn't taught for the last fifteen years who knows nothing about your context as a teacher in Coquitlam can issue a document that essentially improves the work you do. What's even worse is when you get a [Premier Mike] Harcourt or a [Minister of Education Art] Charbonneau who have never ever taught, who know nothing about it, prescribing in some detail what teachers should be doing and making calls which sound good in the press but they don't mean anything to teachers."

PROFESSIONAL DEVELOPMENT

Instead of simply mandating changes, the Education Ministry should have worked harder on encouraging changes through more in-service education, new curriculum materials, opportunities to try Year 2000 methods in pilot programs. But the ministry misconstrued the nature of the change. "They thought it was a curricular or structural change and what should have been obvious to them was it was a professional development challenge," says Roland Case, SFU's representative on the intermediate steering committee. "They spent ages retooling these documents and not getting them right instead of going directly for long-term teacher development and teacher education."

Case says the formidable challenge in any attempt at improving teachers' practice is re-education, as Sarason points out. "It's not getting them to implement this change, it's getting them to change themselves," Case argues. "Getting teachers to integrate more is not a matter of simply reformatting the curriculum documents. They [ministry staff] arbitrarily lumped subjects into four strands . . . and they think by that fiat alone teachers will now be able to draw the connections between the subjects."

"The problem is you can't mandate something like that," says Sonia O'Connor, who has taught at two Vancouver elementary schools that spearheaded Year 2000 techniques, University Hill and Charles Dickens. "You can't go to people and say, 'You're no longer going to teach like this.' Unless you're going to train them differently, it's not going to work." She says that change is more successful when it starts in one place and spreads because others see that it works.

The need for solid professional development was all but ignored in the Year 2000 program. The ministry considered curriculum development more important than professional development, program documents as more important than the quality of teaching. An education adage says, "A good teacher can compensate for a pretty poor curriculum but an excellent curriculum can't compensate for a poor teacher."

Typically, what passed for professional development during Year 2000 were one-shot lectures. They work for telling teachers about changes to the substance of a particular curriculum, grade 7 math for instance, but one-shot lectures aren't enough to teach teachers a different way of looking at education, as was the case for Year 2000.

The irony is that the government was warned of the danger of top-down reform before it embarked on Year 2000. Wrote Ronald Marx and Tarry Grieve in 1988, "It is not productive to decide at a central bureaucracy level how people should teach and then tell them to teach in that manner. Regardless of the desires of senior policy officials, such 'top-down' approaches to teacher reform simply do not work. Top-down reform has been attempted many times and there are virtually no documented successes in the literature. It is far better to engage teachers in the critical reappraisal of their own work and to provide them with the resources, including access to specialists and to other teachers, that will enable them to improve." [7]

PUBLIC OPINION AND POLITICS

Fullan's and Sarason's scholarly works detail the key problems with reform. But these books, as with most of the academic literature on education reform, fall short by failing to address one important issue: politics. Education is a political issue and, as a result, so is education reform. Not only do the change-makers need to ensure that staff accept the proposed reforms, the public must accept them as well or else in the political feedback loop that is democracy, the people at the top—the politicians—will extinguish the reforms with one quick puff. By ignoring the need to communicate to the public, the academic literature on education change assumes that the school system exists in a vacuum and that the political leaders in charge of the reforms don't have a stake in the way the public perceives the changes.

The Year 2000 story is a lesson in the effect of public opinion on education change. The problems began, as explained in this chapter, not because the program was bad for kids but because the government poorly articulated the program and failed to follow through on a public communication plan. Perhaps Year 2000 could have survived all the factors listed earlier in this section. But it wasn't going to survive an antagonistic electorate with a thirst for budget cutting and a distaste for new program spending.

1. Jane Flick et al., "Year 2000 Faculty of Arts Report," unpublished document, University of British Columbia, November 1990.

2. Sarason, Seymour B., *The Predictable Failure of Education Reform*, p. 68.

3. Ibid., p. 101.

4. Ibid., p. 90.

5. Recall my argument in Chapter 2 that the Royal Commission recommendations implied smashing the traditional power relationships in schools. Why the BCTF did not embrace this is baffling.

6. Fullan, Michael G., *The New Meaning of Educational Change*, p. 353.

7. Marx and Grieve, op. cit., p. 92.

[7]
"THE REPORT CARD ON YEAR 2000 IS IN AND IT'S FAILED."

The air in September always seems fresh and new, ironic considering that autumn, the season when grass browns and trees lose their leaves, is just around the corner. Maybe it's because the fall is also a time of new beginnings. The schools once again fill with students wearing new clothes, bearing new notebooks, meeting new teachers. The halls, chalkboards, and lockers are clean. Every school year begins with a fresh slate and a sense of limitless possibility.

Our society is influenced by the school calendar in many ways: programs that took a hiatus for the summer gear up again, people come back to work from vacations. We all notice the start of school and the return of yellow buses to the roads. September is a time when people talk about school.

All of this means it's an opportune time for a politician to catch the public's attention on issues related to education. That's what Premier Mike Harcourt did in September 1993.

"To put it bluntly, the report card on Year 2000 is in and it's failed the grade," said the premier in a front-page story in the

Vancouver Sun on September 4, the Saturday before classes resumed. In case anyone didn't get the message, Harcourt reiterated his point in radio interviews and at the Legislature on September 7, the first day of school, telling reporters that Year 2000 would be replaced by a new emphasis on the basics.

It would be easy to dismiss the premier's statement as just one more of the thousands of comments politicians make on any number of subjects over the years. But it's impossible to overestimate the impact on the education system of those few words. To this day, people in the school system remember them vividly. When I asked people about the premier's comments, dozens responded by shaking their heads in dismay, rolling their eyes in exasperation, or speaking with anger in their voice. No one in the B.C. school system needs to be prompted about what the premier said—just ask, "What did you think of Harcourt's announcement in September '93?" and they know what you're talking about.

"I was disgusted. I truly was," says Jackie Tegart, then-president of the BCSTA. "The first day of school—what a tone to set. The Year 2000 has failed? Failed to what? It was only in the primary grades. He demoralized the system with that one announcement. All the people who had bought in, and spent countless hours implementing and doing professional development and serving on provincial committees, were just devastated. All the people who never wanted the change said, 'Told you so.'"

She adds, "I truly resent playing politics with our kids. It should be something that is above politics. Our young people are too important to be played games with. I'm really tired of governments who think they have to put their stamp on everything. If the NDP government wanted certain changes within the Year 2000 direction, stand up and say so but don't demoralize the system and politicize it like they did. I have never seen a start to school like that year."

"The notion that the schools are not teaching basic skills is just nonsense," says UBC dean of education Nancy Sheehan, calling Harcourt's statement "an abomination . . . a slap in the face to everyone in the education system."

Roland Case of the intermediate steering committee calls it "a repudiation of a tremendous amount of good will on teachers' part. It should have been handled in a more gracious way, far more sensitive to the thousands of good teachers, because they were the ones who caught the spirit of trying to make the system work better for kids. That little act was stupid and foolish."

Although it had rarely praised Year 2000 before Harcourt's announcement, the BCTF rushed to condemn the premier. "The extent to which decisions about education became politically motivated was really clear in that September '93 announcement by Harcourt," says then-president Ray Worley. "Rather than attempting to take on the challenge of making the adjustments, explaining it to the public, taking a step back and assessing it, there was this purely political announcement by Harcourt."

"I never heard in such a short term, so many negative reactions from teachers," says the BCTF's Peter McCue. "I think that was a very poor choice by the premier. The timing of it couldn't have been worse. It undermined a lot of work that many teachers—especially the primary teachers—had been putting in for a number of years. It also undermined the work that a lot of people had begun at the intermediate and secondary level. That comment became divisive: people who were reluctant to change, it made them say, 'See, we told you we were right.' Others felt betrayed."

"The one true surprise in the last number of years was this statement right out of the blue, that the Year 2000 has failed," says North Vancouver superintendent Robin Brayne. "It caught everybody by surprise. People knew that there were some problems with inertia or lack of momentum or lack of focus or anything substantive happening with the Year 2000, but I believe at least in the education community and among many, many parents the ideas of the Year 2000—of how schools should be organized, how instruction should be provided, how we are responsible for the success of each and every learner—were very important principles."

Adds Brayne, "When Mr. Harcourt said the Year 2000 was a failure, the first question anybody would ask was, 'Isn't that a bit of a generalization? Specifically what? The primary program? The resource guides? The philosophy of the graduation program? What aspect of it?' [It caused] great dishevelment in the system for the longest period of time. There was this sense of—if the Year 2000 has failed and that's been the thing everybody's been talking about for the last three or four years—what's going to replace it? What's the vision guiding the system, what's the philosophy, what's the pedagogical model?"

Even the soon-to-be-former Education Minister Anita Hagen didn't like what the premier said. "I've never supported that statement, and in fact, during the last two weeks of my ministry there were dozens of letters and phone calls from people telling us what they were doing and why it was good for kids."

However, Harcourt's statement worked. Education was in the

news every day for two weeks after his announcement. The resulting perception among the public was that he'd killed Year 2000—the message he wanted to send. Most media pundits said he was showing "leadership" by axing the program and criticizing the system for not teaching basic skills.

The reaction that Harcourt didn't expect was an impassioned defence of Year 2000 not just by educators but by parents as well. The response forced some back-pedalling from the government— "We didn't mean to say the basics aren't being taught, we didn't mean to imply that Year 2000 was all bad." But the mission had already been accomplished, the rug had been pulled out from under the Year 2000.

PUBLIC-OPINION POLLING

Harcourt's justification for killing Year 2000 was a Decima Research poll commissioned by cabinet. Based on this poll, the premier cited widespread concern about the school system. "It's a pretty overwhelming opinion out there," he said. "Those concerns are deeply felt and real, and I share them." [1]

The poll indicated that 43 percent of British Columbians felt the school system had "become worse" in the previous five years. Two-thirds of respondents said there is a "great need" to improve the school system and another 30 percent said there is "somewhat" of a need. The three elements most cited as needing improvement were: acquiring basic skills, meeting the needs of all students (not just those who go to university), and preparing kids for the 21st century.

Other key findings cited by Decima included: opposition to Year 2000 was highest among respondents who said they knew a lot about the program; 39 percent of those who knew something about Year 2000 said it would make the system worse; explaining elements of the program made two-thirds feel no different or worse about it; 75 percent of parents felt it would be acceptable to reintroduce letter grades on the report cards of their primary-aged children.

All of this prompted Decima to conclude: "While there is widespread demand for improvements and a strong feeling that the system is not adapting for the next century, the Year 2000 reforms are clearly not seen as part of the solution. In fact, based on these results, the public and parents believe that the reforms are part of the problem. There is substantial support, in fact, for a thorough overhaul of the reforms." [2]

The report continued: "Given this mood, the Ministry is not dealing with a simple communications problem that can be dealt with through a more effective communications campaign in which the reforms are explained. The Ministry is dealing with a public and with parents who believe the reforms are a step in the wrong direction. This is despite the fact that for many elements of the program, such as the integration of subjects, there is considerable support." [3]

But many of the results in the report, obtained under the Freedom of Information legislation, contradict Decima's conclusions and indicate that the results do not imply the need to kill Year 2000. In addition, there are factors contributing to respondents' answers that were ignored.

♦ Frankly, asking people whether the school system needs improvement is like asking people whether they would like to earn more money—who's going to say no? The fact that the affirmative response to this was so high is no surprise and is no indictment of Year 2000.

♦ Almost two-thirds of respondents said they had heard "nothing at all" (40 percent) or "not too much" (22 percent) about the Year 2000. Only one-third of the public knew in which grades the program had been implemented. In other words, ignorance about Year 2000 was far greater than criticism about it.

♦ Among those who had heard "something" or "a lot" about Year 2000, only 30 percent had direct experience through a child—the rest had "heard or read" about it. Even among parents, most had only a second-hand understanding about Year 2000—49 percent of parents of primary children and 66 percent of parents of kids in grades 4 through 12. Obviously, criticisms were mostly based on second-hand information, including media coverage and coffee-shop talk. Also, the report downplayed the finding that one-third of respondents felt more positive about the program after it was explained to them. Considered together, these two factors contradict the conclusion that a communications plan could not improve public opinion.

♦ People's response to Year 2000 was linked to attitudes about the school system. Among those who said schools have become worse in the last five years, 67 percent said Year 2000 cannot be fixed and 30 percent said the program needs many changes. This prompted one of the biggest flaws in the poll: Decima interpreted that attitudes about Year 2000 encouraged the negative impression of the quality of schooling. There is no justification for this. The causal relationship is more likely the other way—someone's global beliefs about the system would impact their opinion of an element within that system. In other words, people's negative feelings toward the quality of education—feelings that people have had for years, as other polls show—would likely cause them to indict Year 2000. The pollsters even wrote, "While it is difficult in the above relationship to determine the extent and the direction of causality . . . the results are highly suggestive that attitudes toward the Year 2000 program have a significant impact on the way the public and parents view public education." [4] That defies logic and is just plain bad science.

- Although 39 percent of the public felt Year 2000 would make the system worse, 35 percent said it would make the system better. That's far from definitive.

- People's dissatisfaction with secondary schools was greater than dissatisfaction with elementary schools. Year 2000 had of course not been implemented in the secondary schools, so if people weren't happy with the upper grades, it wasn't Year 2000 that bothered them, it was the status quo.

- A damning factor that isn't even mentioned as possibly influencing people's answers: the poll was conducted from April 29 to May 16, and at that time, as discussed in Chapter 5, the province was in the middle of a spring full of teacher strikes. Generally, people are not happy with the school system when kids are home from school because of a labour dispute. There's no question that this influenced people's mood about everything related to education, including Year 2000, yet the pollsters and the government chose to ignore that fact.

The Decima poll is far less conclusive than the premier made it out to be. Closer analysis of the poll belies his claims of widespread opposition to Year 2000. It all boils down to this simple idea: if only 38 percent of the public knows something or a lot about the programs and only 39 percent of those feel the program would make the system worse, my calculator tells me that's only 15 percent of the electorate—less than the percentage of people who voted Socred in the last election. Should the government respond so drastically to such a minority?

To put Decima's June 1993 poll in context, it's worthwhile to examine another government-commissioned poll—one that was not publicized—that I also obtained through a Freedom of Information request. Longwoods International conducted a survey in February 1992 that mimics some of the Decima poll's findings: a solid one-third of the public who felt the quality of education had dropped in recent years, limited awareness of Year 2000, strong feelings that kids should obtain basic skills in school. This poll differed from the 1993 survey on two major points: greater support for Year 2000—half of those who were aware of the program felt it would improve the quality of education—and the finding that explaining elements of the problem made only a handful feel worse about Year 2000. In addition, the survey found that experience with Year 2000 tended to increase people's support for it.

The most important finding of this poll was the advice it offered to the Education Ministry. Had it been heeded, it would have minimized the backlash against Year 2000. The pollsters found that people's priorities focused on a general desire to improve the quality of education. In addition, the poll found that the public equated quality with basics and standards. The implication for the ministry: if Year 2000 was to be accepted by the public, they must perceive that the reforms will not sacrifice basics and standards. "The public is quite open to liberal methods of implementation, but only if the basics are taught and standards are met," said the report. "Most are willing to leave the choice of method to education experts so long as the bottom-line outcomes are achieved." [5]

Longwoods made suggestions for ministry communications plans. The most important of these said communications should avoid the semantic trap of portraying learner-focused instruction as the opposite of basics and standards. In addition, the report said that since there is consensus among the public on desired outcomes but not on teaching methods, and since the public tends to judge quality on the basis of results and outcomes, not philosophy or methodology, the ministry should emphasize the benefits of Year 2000 rather than its features.

"Improving public opinion about the education system will require a sustained and consistent program of communications," said the report. "The Ministry must position itself as being committed to improving education quality—not to education reform. Reform implies that what has been done previously is all wrong, thereby undermining public confidence." [6]

What happened to the "sustained and consistent" communication plan? Why didn't the ministry explain that Year 2000 did not mean abandoning basics and standards? The potential pitfalls were spelled out in black and white more than a year before the Decima poll was conducted, yet the government paid no heed.

My Freedom of Information request turned up a poll per year on education since 1988. Common themes in these included: limited awareness among the public of the school reforms, strong emphasis on the importance of the basics, and similar responses when asked to rate the quality of education compared with five years earlier: on average, one-third of respondents said schools had become worse, one-quarter said they've improved, and 40 to 45 percent said they've stayed the same. The 1993 Decima poll should not have come as a big surprise to the government.

ENTER ART CHARBONNEAU

When Mike Harcourt shuffled his cabinet on September 15, no one was surprised to see Anita Hagen get the boot. Somewhat more surprising was his choice of replacement: Kamloops MLA Art Charbonneau, until then Highways Minister. But the choice of Charbonneau made sense: he projected the no-nonsense, businesslike approach that Harcourt wanted to cultivate for his government, he comes from a key bellwether riding that the NDP would love to keep, and he'd done a workmanlike job of keeping his Highways portfolio out of controversy. The public image the government wanted to portray concentrated on his professional background: as a civil engineer, he could be a credible face for the NDP's emphasis on technology and skills in the school system for the new economy.

The views of three vastly different people in the Kamloops education community are a good sampling of opinion about Charbonneau. School board chairman John O'Fee says Charbonneau sets a course and follows it, hasn't been afraid to upset the BCTF, and appears to have a firm grasp of what's happening within the system.

Rick Turner, past-president of the Kamloops District Teachers' Association uses words like hard-working, honesty, and integrity.

Superintendent Tarry Grieve contrasts the new minister's leadership to Hagen's: Charbonneau would say, "I value your input, but now I'll make a decision," while Hagen could never seem to make a decision.

A common theme in people's assessment of Charbonneau is that he looks at schools and the system like an engineer. He's a rational straight arrow, who doesn't have the passion of Tony Brummet but is the sensible and level-headed leader that education needs right now. In the history books, he won't be labelled a great education minister, but he won't be accused of screwing up, either.

Charbonneau likes to show decisiveness and authority and he tries to project it in his words by using the first-person singular whenever he can. His firm determination to erase the ghost of indecisiveness that was Anita Hagen may be his fatal flaw. In his attempts to be decisive, his "I did it my way" approach could mean that the wrong decisions get made. After all, education is not a cut-and-dried affair, like bridge-building.

On November 16, Charbonneau announced the first of his decisions on education reform. The government called it *Improving the Quality of Education in B.C.*, stealing the words directly from a phrase highlighted in the 1992 Longwoods poll and research report. The government set three goals for education: strong basic skills; a common core of learning; more students graduating. "More emphasis on basics, standards and evaluation," said Premier Harcourt in a news release. Needless to say, this was a substantial shift away from the mandate statement that followed the Royal Commission.

These were the visible changes. The ministry sensibly returned to the standard grade designations of kindergarten to 12. "Anecdotal" reports were replaced by "structured written reports." (The difference between the two? My only guess is that a structured written report is a well-written anecdotal report.) Letter grades were revived in the intermediate years—sort of. (The government said letter grades must be issued by teachers but "school districts will determine how those letter grades are communicated to parents.") Accountability was "strengthened" by mandatory school accreditation (which was already widespread throughout the system) and by requiring districts to publish graduation rates and exam scores in their annual reports (remnants of the ghost of the other Hagen—Stan). Finally, the documents released by the ministry included no references to "Year 2000." The announcements did not say the name had officially been dropped, but it was conspicuous by its absence—like a disgraced Soviet general who did not appear on the podium one May Day and whose name was never to be spoken again, as if he'd never existed.

The substantive changes to instruction were few. Letter grades had never been eliminated at the secondary level. Report cards weren't changed: teachers were merely given better guidelines about how to write good ones. Although the official announcements didn't say so, Harcourt and Charbonneau told reporters they would keep the "best" parts of Year 2000.

Yet at the same time, the tone was one of standards and basics.

Reports by Keith Baldrey and Vaughn Palmer of *The Vancouver Sun* indicated that the premier's office had to fight with the Education Ministry bureaucracy to make the changes it wanted. Palmer wrote an account of a meeting between superintendents and Oscar Bedard, assistant deputy minister for education programs, on September 16. There was no indication from this meeting that the ministry planned to back away from any but a few elements of Year 2000, wrote Palmer. In fact, a communications strategy to restore confidence was on the way.

Baldrey wrote that sources told him the ministry was "stubborn and combative." But he said new deputy minister Cynthia Morton (a labour lawyer from Ontario who replaced Valerie Mitchell, turfed the same day as Anita Hagen) "whipped it into shape."

So was the new approach a PR move or a real change to the system? Does the new direction reflect Year 2000 principles or not? I'll address this question later in the chapter.

For his part, Charbonneau certainly wants the public to feel he has fixed things. When I interviewed him this past April in the Vancouver cabinet office at Canada Place, he was firm in his opposition to the perceived problems of Year 2000, even if they were flaws that weren't part of the program's properly expressed philosophy. He disagreed with "those proponents who said you must never criticize a child, that that's harmful to their self-esteem and therefore report cards talk only about what a child can do." He said he doesn't believe that a child will master work if allowed "to work at his or her own pace." And he said the concept of failure has its place in education.

On the names of the grades: "When Grandma said, 'What grade are you in?' the kid wasn't going to reply, 'I'm in the third year of a four-year ungraded primary.'" Charbonneau visited some forty elementary schools and he says all teachers but two described their classes in terms of "grades," and one who called it P2 was corrected by a fellow teacher as it was actually P3.

On report cards: "You've got to inform the parents as accurately as possible, as concisely as possible, with no jargon, as to how their children are doing. If a child is behind where they should be —without trying to pigeonhole them, because indeed children do learn at their own pace, you've got to allow for that—but if the teacher understands quite clearly that the child is having difficulty with reading, then let's inform the parent of that explicitly."

On letter grades: "Here the ardent supporter of the Year 2000 is of the view that letter grade, any kind of measurement, tests, should not be, that you must evaluate the child through the work in the classroom and the so-called portfolio, that a letter grade, a measurement must never be attached. Again, I disagree. And I just cannot believe that the simple provision of a letter grade in and of itself destroys the psyche or destroys the self-esteem of a child. The parents clearly like letter grades, they clearly did not like a two-page jargon-laden can-do report card and they did not want that style extended on up into the intermediate years."

He feels he made the right choices. "I'm getting extremely positive feedback on the report cards and the letter grades. I tried to find some compromise positions to capture the best of both. For example, the written report: a teacher can convey to the parents much more, much richer information about the child than just by letter grades. . . . For the parent who likes to see a bit more structure and a bit more accountability in the system, they have a brief jargon-free written report but they also have the letter grade to give them a snapshot of how their child is doing."

Charbonneau is right about everything except equating letter grades with accountability. As everyone who's ever had a report card knows, one teacher's C is not the same as another teacher's C.

"What does an A tell you? Then tell me what you learned from a portfolio when you go through two months of work and your child talks to you and tells you what he learned," says trustee Jackie Tegart. "What an A told me was that I was a darned good parent. It never told me what he learned."

"I don't see anything beneficial to letter grades," says former deputy minister Sandy Peel. "It's a very, very subjective type of grading. . . . The biggest reason they brought them back in is because we have a whole populace out there that has gone through school having letter grades. It is what they understand, it is what they're comfortable with." He says when his three children brought home report cards, they sometimes would receive a C not because their work was only satisfactory, but because the teacher thought they needed a shake-up. "I sort of guessed that an A was maybe okay. But I discovered later that it was only because they did well relative to the rest of the kids in the class and they really didn't master the material whatsoever." He agrees that it's essential to make written or anecdotal reports meaningful, with benchmarks, and adds that it takes teachers a long time to write good, clear report cards. There's no question that before September 1993, many teachers were writing bad ones—filled with jargon, sometimes making no sense, saying nothing about what the student needed to do to improve.

What Charbonneau says were the changes—the names of the grades, "structured written" reports, and letter grades a few years earlier than proposed—are far from profound. In fact, they're only superficial. If that was all that changed and the rest of Year 2000 remained intact—learner-focused instruction, integration, the constructivist philosophy, the idea that children learn in different ways and at different rates—the program's opponents should still be complaining and writing letters to the minister.

New Intermediate and Graduation Programs

In December 1993, Charbonneau released new intermediate and graduation program documents. Again, they were labelled "proposed policy" and response was solicited. But they were substantially different from previous drafts in at least one visible feature: thickness. The intermediate program was sixteen pages long and the graduation program twenty. They had the mark of careful editorial work. The documents looked better, with cleaner layout and type fonts, unlike the hodgepodge structure and scatter-gun typography of the earlier drafts. The jargon was purged. They could be read and understood in less time than the average person spends on the morning paper.

Many elements were common to both programs, including some elements of Year 2000. The most prominent remnants were the three learning principles (active participation, differing ways and rates of learning, personal and group process). In a fairly strong statement, the documents said, "They are intended to guide all aspects of education practice including curriculum development, instructional planning, resource selection, school and classroom organization, assessment, evaluation and reporting." The intermediate program added, "Flexibility in school organizations and teaching practices will provide an environment that accommodates students' differing ways and rates of learning," while the graduation program said this would be accomplished by "providing a variety of learning experiences." Both documents endorsed "a variety of teaching approaches" but added that "students learn best when they are actively engaged in the learning process." The various program goals also remained, but intellectual development received top billing, de-emphasizing social and career development.

In both programs, the traditional basics were stressed and standards were emphasized, while Year 2000 philosophy appeared to be tacked on. "The Province has set high goals and standards for all students while not expecting that each will achieve them in the same way or at the same time. The Intermediate (or Graduation) Program is based on the belief that all students can learn and succeed and that no student should leave school without the knowledge and skills that are needed for work, community life or further learning."

The documents included a mixed bag of regulations for report cards. The programs endorsed letter grades, but said they must describe what a student can do relative to "expected outcomes," not relative to the rest of the class. Both programs called for "increased use" of portfolios, student-led conferences, peer assessment, and self-assessment, while percentage marks were made mandatory in the graduation program.

The proposals also saw the debut of a new letter grade and the disappearance of the letter F. "IP"—for "in progress"—was to be given when a student had not yet achieved expected learning outcomes. It was an intelligent choice—a subtle endorsement of the idea of continuous progress yet it refused to use the controversial words "no failure."

The final departure from Year 2000 common to both programs was a new course called "Personal Planning." It usurped the Learning for Living curriculum, a core course featuring health, sex education, abuse prevention, and lifestyle issues that was heavily criticized by fundamentalist Christian groups. It also incorporated the ideas of a personal "mentor," as recommended in the Royal Commission to minimize the alienation of the big secondary school where students see multiple teachers. In addition, teachers would offer advice to students on future course selection and career plans, and with their help, students would develop "learning plans." The idea was to encourage students to set immediate and long-term goals and figure out how to achieve them through course selection and career development activities. In addition, it would teach time management, responsibility, and self-assessment.

INTERMEDIATE PROGRAM   The lengthy intermediate program was broken down into three more closely related time periods—grades 4 to 6; 7 and 8; and 9 and 10. It allowed the program to be delineated in a way that reflects the reality of changing adolescents, with an emphasis on skills and content that grows over the years.

The sensitive topic of failing was dealt with in one paragraph and in noncommittal language: "Decisions regarding placement in grades or courses should be made jointly by educators and parents or guardians in consultation with students. This will provide a positive and flexible approach to help students reach their full potential." Also, the document endorsed integration but left its use up to the teacher.

GRADUATION PROGRAM The program divided grade 11 and 12 into "foundation studies" and "elective studies." The staples of existing graduation requirements remained: English 11 and 12, Social Studies 11, a math course, and a science course. Additional requirements included two credits (half a course) each in fine arts and either physical education or "practical arts" (in other words, business ed, home ec, industrial ed). Four credits of career and personal planning were also made mandatory: two credits per year, including one mandatory credit (thirty hours of instruction time) devoted to some form of work experience, which had been put forward in Year 2000 drafts. The Socred-induced "Consumer Education" course (derisively referred to as learning how to consume) was replaced by a course called "Society and the Individual," seen by critics as an NDP version of civics. The total for foundation studies was thirty-two credits (equivalent to eight full-year courses, two more than previously mandated), leaving twenty-four credits of electives. Integration was not even mentioned, let alone recommended.

THE K-12 EDUCATION PLAN

In response to its request for feedback on the 1993 drafts of the intermediate and graduation programs, the ministry heard from more than 16,000 people—seven times the number of submissions to the Royal Commission.

In September 1994 in a Burnaby classroom, Mike Harcourt and Art Charbonneau released—finally—real, live government policy. Not a draft proposal, but policy. It bore the innocuous name "The Kindergarten to Grade 12 Education Plan," evidence that the government did not wish to be burned by people associating the system's problems with a catchy label like Year 2000.

The main document summarized all three programs yet was a thin twenty pages. It was designed for general consumption, along with two even shorter documents, *Report to Parents* and *Parents' Guide to Standards*. For the field, policies were laid out in more detail in four further documents: *Implementation Resource Part 1: Guidelines for the Kindergarten to Grade 12 Education Plan; Implementation Resource Part 2: Instructional Strategies and School*

Organization; Guidelines for Student Reporting; Putting Policies Into Practice Implementation Guide.

In most respects, the plan showed little change from the December 1993 drafts. This final version of the policy dropped the proposal for a mandatory "Society and the Individual" civics course from the graduation program and incorporated elements of it into Social Studies 11, while it made fine arts mandatory from grades 4 through 10 and a second language mandatory from grades 5 to 8.

Report-card guidelines were altered somewhat. Two "informal" report cards were mandated in addition to the structured written reports. These could be as much as a student-led conference or portfolio (as urged in the previous drafts) or as little as a phone call—the choice was left to teachers. Also, the *Guidelines for Student Reporting* document contained information that should have been issued in the first days of anecdotal reporting: concrete examples of how to write a meaningful report card.

The letter F returned to grade 11 and 12 report cards, along with C+ and C-, because the proposed percentage range of the C grade was so wide—50 to 72 percent. Regulations for the use of the IP grade were included: when teachers give a student an IP, they must state what needs to be done to reach the expected standard and state a deadline for meeting the requirements.

The K-12 plan included some subtle shifts in emphasis from the drafts. Grade placement received far more attention than the cursory treatment of the 1993 program proposals, yet the guiding philosophy was more vague and noncommittal than even the drafts: "In grades 4 to 12, the decision for a student to advance or repeat a grade will be made in the best interest of that student by the teachers, parents, and the school principal. In making placement decisions, those involved should consider the available research, the age of the student, and the intervention support available." Of course, that's what has been done for years.

Accompanying this was less emphasis on students' different rates and ways of learning, although the idea retained its place in the three learning principles. That sent a mixed message: Is that principle important or not?

Finally, a new theme in the K-12 plan was applied studies. In harmony with the government's Skills Now program—promoting links between the workplace and schools, colleges, and universities—the government announced it would revamp secondary-school curricula "to put more emphasis on the practical applications of learning." The goal was to answer the criticism that schools weren't preparing kids for the working world nor meeting the needs of students who don't attend university.

And the government sent a firm message on the time line: the new curriculum requirements would take effect in September 1995.

ANALYSING THE NEW PROGRAMS

The program documents are obviously miles ahead of their Year 2000 versions in clarity. They get away from the vague language of previous drafts and state how changes will be made: with new curricula all around, each incorporating the so-called "new basics" of problem-solving and computer use.

The reissued documents were "good sound pieces of work: simple, straightforward, practical advice to people about what this is all about and how to get on with it," says Jack Fleming, who was the ADM responsible for the Year 2000 program documents. "Some of it is incongruous, but you buy some of that in a system that's politically driven. To a large degree I think they're doing the right thing."

Most people in the system are satisfied with marks that compare students' performance to outcomes ("criterion-referenced"). It allows for the letter grades that make parents happy yet isn't based on direct comparisons of one child to another ("norm-referenced").

Personal planning is important because it recognizes and instills the importance of goal-setting and course selection by formalizing the process. If teachers take their mentoring role to heart, it will help reduce the likelihood that students get lost in the shuffle of a big school. Its manifestation in the early grades is a little questionable, however. Why does the program say the primary curriculum is designed to "develop traits and attitudes that contribute to career awareness and development"? These are kids who say they want to be baseball players and astronauts when they grow up. This is taking the idea of school as workplace training ground way too far. Still, it doesn't take away from the importance of planning in the older grades.

There has been mixed response to the required extra fine arts and practical arts courses: some like it as a symbol that these things are important in our society, others say forcing kids to take more courses they may not want contradicts the goal of relevance and goes against the Royal Commission recommendation for more flexibility on course selection.

The official line from the ministry is that the new plan is more reflective of the Royal Commission than Year 2000 was. A ministry bureaucrat points with pleasure to Tony Brummet's January 1989 announcement of policy directions stemming from the commission because it shows the same themes as the K-12 plan: problem-solving, creative thinking, reaffirming the importance of literacy, expanded use of technology. "It's back on track," he says.

That's also what people who served on the Royal Commission like to say. Valerie Overgaard of the curriculum research team comments, "Making things more flexible, trying to find ways to make learning more relevant, real-life applications, criterion-referenced assessment, credit for outside work reflect our recommendations. There's less of the fuzzy constructivist notions of themes and multi-age grouping."

IMPLEMENTATION   The NDP's changes to the system have, however, revived the complaints of too much, too fast. Change has been in the works for years for the secondary grades, notes a ministry official, but staff were sceptical it would ever become reality and that's why they're complaining.

But schools did have something to gripe about. They didn't get a draft of the personal planning curriculum until March 1995, usually a time of year when students have already started selecting next year's courses and school timetables are being designed. Principals were not only wondering how to rearrange their rigid timetables to fit it in, but how to deliver this unfamiliar new animal. The newly revised kindergarten to grade 7 curricula—in a new format known as integrated resource packages—arrived in mid-April, also to be implemented in the fall.

North Vancouver superintendent Robin Brayne says the implementation time line is somewhat unrealistic. "Look at all these changes and see what a grade 6 teacher has to come to grips with in the next three years": new language arts, social studies, math and science curricula, along with a recommendation to use more information technology. And transcending it all are new policies on reporting and assessment, special education, heritage languages, aboriginal issues, English as a second language. "It's a shame, because the substantive changes are good," says Brayne.

WORK EXPERIENCE AND APPLIED CONTENT IN ACADEMIC COURSES
The idea of applied academics deserves a nod of commendation. Since the Royal Commission, everyone in the B.C. school system parroted the statement that schools must do a better job for kids who don't go to university. But nothing tangible was being done about it except further statements affirming this need. Increasing the applied content of courses and reviewing the split between "English" on the academic side and "Communications" on the vocational

side is a laudable step. How it will work in practice remains to be seen, once the curriculum guides are revised and teachers begin to teach from them.

UBC associate dean of education Jane Gaskell, whose research has focused on work experience and the school-to-work transition, likes the impetus behind the graduation program because it gives legitimacy and credibility to the world of work. "I think it has a lot to do with Charbonneau as a person," says Gaskell. "As an engineer, he understands the importance of what he calls skills or more applied practical kinds of knowledge and he wants to get that into the schools. What schools count as knowledge has to be broadened and should include a notion of the outside world, the real, applied, practical problem-solving knowledge."

But she's concerned that the changes will continue to ghettoize kids in the non-academic or vocational stream. The solution is to include more applied content in the academic courses, says Gaskell. The difficulty is getting universities to accept such courses for entrance.

Work experience gets a more mixed reception. Although it's universally welcomed as a way to make school seem more relevant to teens who don't plan to go to university, making it mandatory for those who are driven in their post-secondary education goals seems unnecessary.

"In theory it's a good idea, but I have a lot of problems with the way it is going to happen," says Gaskell. She says it shouldn't merely be a requirement that students put in time at work but they must take a critical look at issues in the workplace as well.

In addition, there are plenty of concerns about how work experience will function in practice: Who will monitor or supervise it? What about safety? What variety is there for students in small or one-industry or bedroom communities? What kind of experiences will count—volunteer work, for instance? How will it fit into the rigid timetable? Do businesses know the implications of thousands of kids per year descending on their workplaces? The general consensus is that in the rush to look decisive, the government did not think through all the potential pitfalls.

There is less consensus on the validity of work experience itself. It boils down to a philosophical question: What is the purpose of schooling?

Olav Slaymaker says both objectives—educating citizens and preparing them for the workforce—are equally valid. "We have to be committed to students' careers too. The academic system has resisted that for too long."

Lynn Stephens, the Liberal education critic, says work experience is valuable because it helps students understand the work world: "Be there on time, this is what is expected of you, this is how you dress."

Others aren't ready to jump on the work-experience bandwagon. "I don't doubt that schools should prepare kids for the workforce. But are there other purposes for schools?" asks Kamloops superintendent Tarry Grieve.

"Preparing for jobs is important, but that's not all schools do," says Roland Case of the intermediate steering committee. "We need to prepare people who will vote, people who will live meaningful lives. We can get carried away with the preoccupation on work."

The BCTF has managed to find consensus on this issue—it's opposed to making work experience mandatory. "It's wrong [for government and business] to give the view to parents or the public that somehow schools can prepare kids for jobs because we can't and we never have," says Ken Novakowski. "We give them the basic skills that they need for basic entry-level and intermediate jobs but we don't prepare them for specific jobs We're not a job-training institution in that sense."

This prompts a seldom-tackled question: What does business get out of all this? What does Corporate Canada really mean when it says kids produced by the school system don't fit into the workforce? Their commitment to training students for skills rings hollow when Canadian business invests less than two days per year training the average worker, compared to nearly eight days a year in Germany. Perhaps it's an attempt to pass even more of its training needs on to the public schools and post-secondary institutions. Keith Gray, the B.C. Business Council representative to the graduation steering committee, responds, "We've never said in the business community that schools, colleges, institutes were there to job-train students." [7]

Also at issue is whether in trying to meet the needs of students who don't go to university we are in fact bowing to the god of technology—a technology that will soon become obsolete. Given the conditions noted by the Royal Commission—the pace of change, the number of times people will switch careers, the high sophistication of current technology—and considering the primitive equipment high schools can afford, shouldn't we just give students a good education? A narrow interpretation of skills as "technical" may be counter-productive.

At his most cynical, Charles Ungerleider of UBC thinks the emphasis on skills training is an attempt to cool the demand for places in university, which costs the government a lot of tax dollars. At the same time, he wonders if we are preparing non-academic students for jobs that won't exist in the future, since the traditional trades are shrinking.

Ungerleider also worries that making work experience part of school will heighten the attractiveness of employment "for kids whose view of the future last until the weekend." If they're getting paid and their bosses offer them a few more hours per week, they may wonder why they're going to class. He recalls the late 1970s when lots of kids from Duchess Park Secondary in Prince George quit school to become truck drivers. Now a lot of them are unemployed. He says "socially meaningful" work should be given more consideration—organizing activities for seniors, building playgrounds, meeting the need for school-based day-care by minding younger children, something that's proven to boost a sense of belonging and responsibility among older kids.

INTEGRATED RESOURCE PACKAGES   These are the new one-stop shopping resources for teachers—more than just curriculum guides, they contain course content, suggested teaching methods, print and visual resources to complement the courses, and suggestions on how to assess student mastery. Some people hope these packages will help change some teachers' view of the curriculum as "ground to be covered."

Absorbing all of these curriculum revisions is a lot to expect of teachers, says Jack Fleming. He says he'd be excited if people in the system simply understood the implications of the three learning principles. "If they do that they'll be 85 percent of the way home. To me, that's far more profitable. So somebody ought to be promoting those learning principles, explaining them to people, telling people why they're important, bringing out the research that demonstrates them, pointing to successes where those principles are brought into what schools do. Those are the kinds of things the ministry is not doing well."

THE MIXED MESSAGE OF THE K-12 PLAN

What is the guiding philosophy of "The Kindergarten to Grade 12 Education Plan"? Does it hold true to Year 2000 principles? Does it preach the back-to-basics traditional approach? Both? Neither? It's a question that cannot be answered in either-or terms. Not only does the document itself refuse to wear its heart on its sleeve, its heart seems to be in different places at once. The result is a mixed message to the school system and the public.

As we take a look at the evidence, Exhibit One seems clear. It's the message the government wants to send to the public. Witness the first words of the press releases issued along with the documents: "More structure and a greater emphasis on career planning highlight proposed changes to the intermediate and graduation programs in B.C. public schools." [8] "High standards, clear reporting to parents, a renewed emphasis on the basics and more relevant studies to prepare students for the real world highlight the changes to B.C.'s school system announced today." [9] The government wants people to think "standards, basics, structure, clarity, preparing students for the work world" when they look at the education system. But beware: what the government wants you to believe is not always reality. In fact, it can be the opposite.

Exhibit Two also seems clear, but it contradicts Exhibit One. Although he doesn't trumpet it to the public, Art Charbonneau's official line to people in the school system says that the K-12 education plan is "80 to 90 percent" consistent with Year 2000. "The core of it is still there and will continue to be there. The core of Year 2000 is learning by doing, hands-on, group problems, teamwork, that kind of thing and that's still there. Multi-age grouping is another element that's still there. Many of the sort of pedagogical aspects are intact."

A revealing statement is Charbonneau's answer to my question of why he dropped the name Year 2000. "The things to me that were not central to the philosophy had become the public image of 2000 and had stuck to it. The name became part of the problem. To say to people, 'No, no, we've still got the philosophy, I still support the philosophy, I want to see that philosophy extended as far up through the intermediate as we can get it, I want to take all that positive stuff,' I was not going to make it as long as it was called the Year 2000. It's a public perception thing and I've tried to get around it by saying, 'Fine, we won't use that name.'" The philosophy that "the school is here for the child" is still in place, he says, but he balks at calling it "child-centred" or "learner-centred."

"With rare exception I ran into parents who did other than support what I feel are the core elements of 2000," Charbonneau says. "There are those who would still like to see the kids from grade 1 up lined up in rows and having a lecture-style delivery but those parents are relatively few and far between."

On the other hand, he admits that integration and learner-focused teaching styles aren't recommended for the higher grades. "They will have them as an option," says Charbonneau. "We also have to recognize not only the difference in the child as the child progresses, but we have to recognize the difference in the sets of teachers." If teachers in the upper intermediate grades try integration and it works, their colleagues will follow suit, says Charbonneau. He speculates that in ten years, there will be more integration in use in grades 4 to 7, but it will peter out in grades 8 and 9.

Exhibit Three is an item that sends no message one way or the other: placement. The vague notion in the K-12 plan document of "what's best for the student" says nothing about whether learning should be continuous or whether grade repetition is endorsed. The IP letter grade implies support for continuity, but continuous learning isn't mentioned.

Exhibit Four sends a confusing message. The K-12 document says the three principles of learning form "the foundation of the education program. They guide all aspects of educational practice." But in reality, they don't. The idea that students learn in different ways and at different rates is de-emphasized in the K-12 plan. The 1993 program drafts made important statements about the implications of the principles for classroom practice: that students learn best when they're actively engaged, for instance—but those statements don't appear in the K-12 plan. Also gone are the notions that all students can learn and succeed, that intermediate students need "supportive environments that emphasize caring, trust, order and security," that co-operative learning works well, and that integration helps students make connections between the world and subjects and between discrete disciplines.

So, does the K-12 plan reflect the principles of Year 2000? It depends on whom you ask.

On the yes side, there are two former ministry officials who supported Year 2000, Sandy Peel and Jack Fleming.

Peel says the government seems to have a commitment to its basic principles. "The essence of what was being attempted is there. I think what they're trying to do is package it in a more traditional way that doesn't raise the same fears of certain teacher groups, parents, etc."

"If you ask most people who know what the government has now done, most people will tell you it's about 85, 90 percent consistent with what we always thought we'd do in the first place," says Fleming. "There are particulars which some of us would argue are not consistent but when you're looking at a whole huge system like education, the fact that some parts aren't consistent with the others shouldn't come as any great surprise to anybody." He says the career and personal planning program is a strong mechanism that focuses on the learner.

On the no side are Year 2000 supporters Larry Kuehn of the BCTF and SFU professors Roland Case and Milt McClaren.

The principles of learning are de-emphasized and the active learning talked about in the integrated resource packages is a watered-down version of constructivism, argues Kuehn. He also says the type of assessment preached in the intermediate program is a fundamental shift from Year 2000 and will drive teachers away from the methods implied by the learning principles.

A pivotal part of Year 2000 that's been tossed out is integration, says Case. He believes teachers will interpret the emphasis on accountability as even more pressure to cover content. "Covering the content is seen to be the curriculum and critical thinking is the add-on," says Case. "The more explicit the curriculum gets, the more literal and overwhelmed teachers feel about the amount they have to cover." What follows are tests that are preoccupied with retention of information and facts, which choke intellectual development.

The program's emphasis on tough standards is misdirected, because it's like raising the height of the bar in the pole vault, says Case. "People who couldn't get over it before are not going to improve their performance just 'cause it's higher. In fact what happens is it often discourages those who could otherwise get over it. It doesn't in any way address any of the root causes of what will increase performance. What increases performance is better instruction, better teaching. So if they're serious about raising standards they'd improve the quality of pedagogy. The irony is that despite the rhetoric, the strategies presented have now taken money away from [professional development for] teachers. It would have been better placed helping teachers become more effective at improving kids' performance."

Former deputy minister Wayne Desharnais has some problems with the direction taken by the government that fired him. "I don't see the documents reflecting fundamental reform. I see them reflecting some change, but not the kind of fundamental reform we had anticipated as part of the Year 2000 philosophy."

SFU's Milt McClaren calls the NDP's changes a 180-degree turn, "a complete abandonment of educational principles. I think we've really lost our force from the Royal Commission." He notes that people in the ministry say they're staying the course and he applauds some of the efforts, but he feels the system is still struggling to recover from the NDP's decision to kill Year 2000. "You took the most coherent, the most philosophically unified group of teachers in the province, the ones that committed themselves most to the Royal Commission—

namely the primary team—you abandoned them and stabbed them in the back at a political level," says McClaren. He says Harcourt "disgraced those teachers, he threw them on the rubbish heap."

Given all this unclear and contradictory evidence, what is the guiding philosophy of the K-12 plan? Why can't people agree on whether the plan reflects or rejects Year 2000? The key sentence in the K-12 document is, "While the Ministry of Education will determine what students need to learn, districts and schools will determine how they are to learn it." In other words, the program's philosophy is no philosophy—it's left to the vagaries of individual districts, schools, and teachers.

So seven years after Barry Sullivan and crew set out on a mission to improve the quality of education in B.C., we are left with this. All the evidence about how kids learn, the effort at explaining it to teachers and parents and showing educators why it should be applied in schools is for nought? People in the system are supposed to act like it never happened?

But here's the catch: good teachers aren't capable of acting like it didn't happen. Daphne Macnaughton of the intermediate team says a teacher compared the techniques she learned through the Year 2000 proposals to recycling: "I've been recycling for years. And now somebody says I have to start putting my bottles and cans and things back into the garbage. I can't do it. I can't not know what I know. I can't unlearn that because I've moved on. The difficult thing is there's an inspector who's coming around and lifting the lid on the garbage can." The knowledge about how kids learn has taken hold in her brain and regardless of what the government says, she will use Year 2000 techniques in her classes.

Year 2000 principles can be found in bits and pieces scattered across the province. Teachers are using integration, though not because of any ministry decree. They are doing it because it makes sense. Humanities teams are springing up in secondary schools. Student-led conferences, co-operative learning, self-directed learning: Year 2000 gave credence to these things and supported people who wanted to try them, and since they work, they won't be abandoned just because the government offers only lukewarm support. People in education recognize the need for a student-centred school system. And that is why, despite concerted attempts to kill it, Year 2000 is not dead.

"People in the high schools and intermediate [grades] who now have had the experience of being more collaborative or working with fewer kids or trying integrated programs or humanities or whatever those innovative pockets are, those things will mushroom like the primary program did," says Colleen Politano of the primary team.

Year 2000 is alive in schools like Charles Dickens Elementary in East Vancouver, where staff chose as far back as 1988, before the name Year 2000 was ever spoken, to use techniques like multi-age grouping, team teaching, integration, and meeting more than just the intellectual needs of students.

"We feel strongly enough about this that we are going to continue to foster these beliefs regardless of whether or not the Year 2000 is dead," says George Rooney, the school's veteran and widely respected principal.

He's convinced that only a minority of people were opposed to Year 2000 and their criticisms were misguided. "We never got away from teaching basics, teaching phonics, having discipline in schools," he says. "Four years ago, the province took great pride in being on the cutting edge of education in North America. Now it's being condemned for producing graduates who can't read, write, or spell, which I've heard since 1950 when I was in school."

"We're not teaching the kids to be dependent on this system. We're teaching them to be independent learners," says Dickens teacher Karim Bhimani. "We do all of the core subjects, we make sure we're consistent with the kids, we give them homework, we make sure it's not a free-for-all here in terms of discipline."

Ultimately, Rooney believes the government's actions were based on politics, not what's best for kids' education. "What the Year 2000 started was legitimate good teaching and learning practices. The unfortunate thing was that the name became a political label," he says. "It's easy to rally people around a label like Year 2000 and thereby influence people like Harcourt."

In his novel *Hard Times*, Charles Dickens depicted a misguided character named Thomas Gradgrind whose relentless emphasis on the importance of memorizing facts and statistics drove all creativity out of his two children. Dickens might rest easily knowing that the staff at the East Vancouver school named for him continue to fight for a different kind of school philosophy.

---

1. "Harcourt to throw out much of Year 2000 education plan," *Vancouver Sun*, September 8, 1993.

2. "A Decima Research Report to Government of British Columbia, Ministry of Education." Unpublished document, June 1993. Executive summary, p. 28.

3. Ibid., p. 29.

4. Ibid., p. 50.

5.   Longwoods International, "Education Issues in British Columbia." Prepared for the
     B.C. Ministry of Education, May 1992. Unpublished document, pp. 16, 21.

6.   Ibid., pp. 24, 27.

7.   Almanac open-line show, CBC Radio Vancouver, January 26, 1995.

8.   "Intermediate and Graduation Program Policy papers released," news release 36-93,
     B.C. Education Ministry, December 14, 1993.

9.   "Harcourt announces education improvements for 1994," news release 36-94,
     B.C. Education Ministry, September 12, 1994.

[8]
THE TRADITIONAL SCHOOL

Even though Year 2000 is alive, an equally strong movement in British Columbia completely rejects the principles of the program. In 1994, it manifested itself in Surrey when a group of parents asked the school board to create a "traditional" school emphasizing the basics, teacher-directed instruction, and discipline. Although superintendent Doug Jennings recommended against the proposal, noting it would cost the district more than $500,000 extra, trustees gave the plan the thumbs up. The Surrey Teachers' Association slapped an ill-advised "hot edict" on the school, threatening to blacklist teachers who applied there, but the union backed down and the school opened its doors in September.

The birth of Surrey Traditional School is a jumping-off point for a discussion of several interconnected themes: teaching methods, parental involvement in schools, conservative values, the power of unions, choice, charter schools. All of these issues either simmered beneath the surface of the debate over the school or else boiled over.

First and foremost, the parental demand for Surrey Traditional School was in itself a critique of Year 2000 teaching methods. By saying they wanted a back-to-basics school, the people behind the school implied that they felt the basics weren't being taught. They blamed it on Year 2000—even though the premier announced the death of the program the previous September. They felt the neighbourhood schools lacked the orderliness, discipline, and structure necessary for learning.

The traditional-school proposal expressed parental frustration at what they saw as a lack of responsiveness from the system. These parents feel schools are the reverse of jails—their walls are designed to keep people out. They felt their presence was unwelcome in the classroom and their involvement in their children's education was unappreciated.

Analysing Surrey Traditional as an expression of ideology has profound implications. The demand for the school fits into the context of *B.C. Report* and the conservative "quality education" lobby groups. The critics who believed the school would become a white bastion were wrong: a significant number of children with Asian backgrounds attend the school. But its links to religion are strong. Many of the parents who send their children there are fundamentalist Christians. Kids in grade 7 told me that they'll probably attend Christian private schools this fall since Surrey trustees refused to extend the school to grade 8 this year. One of the school's founders, Heather Stilwell, is a former president of the Christian Heritage Party and deputy leader of the Family Coalition Party. Grade 5 teacher Gloria Kieler wants to establish an all-Christian television channel. In fact, the religious overtones of the school prompted one of its founders, John Pippus, to send his children elsewhere. (Pippus is now the parent co-ordinator for the anti-union group Teachers for Excellence.)

The parents who wanted Surrey Traditional marched under the banner of choice. It's a concept that's difficult to disagree with. Who's going to say there should be less choice in the school system? School choice is proving to be the hot education issue of the 1990s.

At the same time, many people who lobby for choice in public schools use another term interchangeably: charter schools. There's a difference. A charter school is not controlled by a public school board. The provincial government grants a charter to a group—be they parents, teachers, coaches, or a mix of the above, and hands them the requisite amount of cash and leaves them to run the school within certain guidelines. As you'll see in the final chapter of this book, the provincial Liberal party has endorsed both charter schools and choice schools and doesn't draw a sharp line between the two.

These are the issues to keep in mind as we visit Surrey Traditional and a handful of other schools in the Lower Mainland.

SURREY TRADITIONAL SCHOOL

More than 200 children are on the waiting list to get into the school, which held 211 students in 1994-95, its first year of existence. The school was overwhelmed with requests for visits, both by parents of prospective students and groups who want to form similar schools elsewhere (and journalists like me), so it restricted such visits to monthly tours. At the beginning of the tour I tagged along with, principal Cathie Paton addressed the people crowded into the staff room and shattered some of their preconceptions when she warns against jumping on the school-bashing bandwagon. "This particular school is no different from any other school in the public school system," said Paton. "When people say this is back-to-basics, that's a misnomer. The basics are taught in all classrooms."

She explains that the essence of the school is a consistent method of instruction: traditional or teacher-centred. She contrasts it to what she calls the "whole-language approach" in which "curriculum is integrated, a lot of games, co-operative learning, read a lot and write a lot."

Although she tells parents the classrooms look similar to what they were like "when you were in school," Paton gives them a long list of things that the Traditional school is not. "This doesn't mean we're going back to the 1950s. This doesn't mean the whole-language teachers do not teach skills or do not teach the basics.... This is not a criticism of the neighbourhood schools. It doesn't mean we're better than the neighbourhood schools. It doesn't mean this works for all children."

She adds, "I think I'm a very good teacher, but I don't think my way is the only way. This is a method that suits some teachers, some kids, and some parents. When that all clicks, you have wonderful learning."

During the tour, various parents say things that hint at their reasons for wanting to send their children to a traditional school.

There's a mother from Sardis who talks continually about her son who obtained 94 percent on a grade 1 achievement test in September, but the school refused to push him ahead. She has since fought "tooth and nail" against the administration.

A mother from Duncan lobbying for a traditional school there says when she went to her child's school, "I found the classroom kind of chaotic. It was the whole-language thing. The kids weren't learning to read."

"I went to a private school and this is the closest thing I've seen to it," comments another woman after observing a few classrooms.

"They spend a lot more time working than playing," says one member of the parent advisory council. Her tone makes it unnecessary to add the implied "unlike the regular schools."

A visitor says when she heard the kids sing the national anthem this morning, "I just wanted to cry."

This adoration of compliant, orderly children comes through often. The mother of a current student gushes that when the children are all standing in rows at an assembly, all dressed in the school uniform of green sweatshirt over white shirt with dark pants or skirts, "They're so beautiful."

"Let me see who's ready to line up," announces grade 3 teacher Tracy Majhen. Obediently, the children sit up straight at their desks, hands folded, eyes to the front. "Joan should not be talking," says Majhen. She waits for silence to descend, surveys the room to see who's fidgeting the least, then announces, "Sammy's row can line up." The kids in that row do so, but not before pushing their chairs in close to their desks. The scene is repeated a row at a time before the children file out of the room to the hallway.

"It's incredible," effuses a prospective student's mother. "I can't believe it. What I really like is the order."

Majhen, only three years out of university, wouldn't look out of place on Commercial Drive in Vancouver with her black leggings and funky silver earrings, but she's conservative in her approach to teaching. In fact, she apologizes as I observe art class because it's "not very traditional."

She says she applied to work at the Traditional school because she found she was using direct instruction most of the time. She says she incorporates some Year 2000-type strategies but leans overall toward traditional methods: she uses textbooks as the framework, repetition, drills, flash cards, and lecture-style presentation. The kids almost always work on their own. "Once you put them in groups, the noise level increases and I don't think much gets done."

Majhen likes the lighter discipline load she carries here. "Parents are very supportive and I'm not dealing with behaviour problems as much. When you don't deal with behaviour problems you can teach so much more." She adds that it would be wonderful to work in a private school.

Parent involvement is paramount at Surrey Traditional. For instance, the education committee of the parent advisory council chose the school's readers. They picked the *Journeys* series over the popular *Impressions* series, which has been a constant source of criticism by fundamentalist Christian groups who don't like the fact that it depicts ghosts. "To a lot of our parents, it is important that they know exactly what is going to be taught," says parent advisory council president Liz Robertson.

The parents group also had concerns about the CARE program, which teaches primary children about "bad touching" as a means of preventing child abuse. But their opposition won't keep it out of classrooms. Paton says parents who don't want their child exposed to it can opt out, but she adds, "I personally believe in the CARE program and I will teach it."

Partnership is the aim of Surrey Traditional, says Paton. "It's the parents' involvement and support that is the key to this school," she continues, but adds that such involvement is not unique. "The public school system has always been open to parents but the perception out there is that it's not."

DISCOVERY ELEMENTARY

On the parental involvement scale, Cathie Paton compares Surrey Traditional to another school in the district that in its teaching approach is the opposite of what the parents at the open house want. In fact, it's what they feel they're escaping from.

Discovery Elementary was established in the early 1970s, and was dismissed by critics as a hippy school. Staff based their philosophy on Adlerian psychology, which states that the social and emotional needs of a child must be fulfilled before intellectual progress can take place.

"It was rough getting going because we were pushing against the stream," recalls primary teacher Suzanne Jennings. "Many of our ideas were pooh-poohed because we were considered too radical."

"Pre-Year 2000, this school was doing a lot of things that would be considered Year 2000: multi-age groupings, themes, co-operative learning, whole-language instruction," says principal Ray Prosser.

Not only are there no desks in straight rows at Discovery, there are no desks period. Classes sit on the floor, sometimes in huddled groups, sometimes in assigned spots around one large circle. Teachers have bookshelves and a table, but they don't lecture to the class from behind them.

But even people with conservative values would have trouble arguing with the school's decision to hold activities that emphasize family: instead of a sports day as the school year ends, Discovery holds a family picnic.

The ideas that Surrey Traditional and Discovery share go further than parental involvement. Both are choice schools, so the parents who send their kids there are interested in and committed to their children's education. Both have enthusiastic and committed teachers and a principal who supports the school's philosophy. Both display children's art on the walls. Both teach phonics, though in different ways. And, perhaps a surprise to some, Discovery is not a noisy circus where kids do whatever they want.

"This school is just as structured as the Traditional school, it's just structured in a different way," says Prosser. People who criticize the Discovery model as lacking structure ought to look at the way the school handles recess and the lunch-hour free time. Before they leave the classroom, each student chooses an activity from a list of options, such as skipping, adventure playground, soccer, etc. The deal is they must stick with that activity for the entire session. "It teaches us that when we make a commitment, we keep the commitment," one grade 5 student explains to me.

In the grade 7 class, all that teacher Charlie Metzger needs to do to announce that it's time for class to begin is switch off the light, and a room full of boisterous kids goes silent. Even at the primary level they're well trained. One by one, as they finish their lunch, the tiny kids in Margaret Buchanan's class stand and wait for her to issue a little hand signal that allows each to be dismissed.

Decisions are made democratically. During my visit, my discussion with Michael Ewen's grade 5-6 class extended into the noon-hour outdoor playtime, so the class voted on whether to keep going. They're a polite bunch, not talking when it's another person's turn. They seemed articulate and confident when asked what makes their school different from others.

"We know five ways of multiplying. They [friends at other schools] know all their times tables. They've memorized them. They just don't really know exactly what it means," says Taegan Hickling, a grade 5 student. "We're allowed to give our opinion on things. In other schools, it's like, 'You have to do this and if you don't like it that's too bad.'"

Teachers say the kids become comfortable relating to adults because of the way teachers and students interact. They experience speaking out, responsibility, independence, all reasons why Discovery kids defy the sceptics who say, "Yes, but they will crumble when they get into the real world." In fact, Surrey school district studies have shown that when they go on to secondary school, students from Discovery achieve higher academically and are more likely to be involved in extracurricular activities than average. There's no doubt that it's related to the higher-than-average parent commitment to education, but it also makes the "back-to-basics" cry ring hollow.

Teachers and parents at this school believe passionately in its philosophy. The parents group presented a brief to the Royal Commission. After Mike Harcourt announced that Year 2000 "failed the grade," the staff fired off an angry letter telling the premier that they had used Year 2000 ideas for years and been very successful, and that perhaps they would be successful elsewhere with a little more commitment and time. After the edict on letter grades came down from Art Charbonneau, the 150-odd parents attending Discovery's annual general meeting voted unanimously that the school maintain its current reporting style and that letter grades—which teachers must calculate according to ministry mandate—are to be given to parents only on request.

"I wanted my children to love learning the way I did before I had it crushed out of me," says Paula Campbell, who has one son in grade 7 at Discovery and an older son who had attended previously. "We [parents] all went to the traditional school form and I found it very demoralizing every time I got a report card because they never focused on what I had done well but they focused on what I had done badly. By grade 7, I didn't want to do anything."

Campbell's oldest son now goes to Relevant private school in Cloverdale, where his marks are As and Bs. Her younger son is in a touring choir and the choir director, remarking about how disciplined the boy is, assumed he attended a strict private school.

"What [Discovery has] given my children is something that will hold them over for the rest of their lives," says Campbell. "They're excited about learning here. That's exactly what learning should be, a pleasure."

"Most of what had gone on in schools for me was quite damaging," says Janice Gale, mother of a grade 7 student. "Most of what we were forced to do was either boring or had nothing to do with my life."

She has no worries about unleashing her supposedly coddled children on the competitive world of the secondary schools. "The elementary years are so crucial. If they've had seven years of positive and encouraging stuff, they're prepared to blend into any situation." Teachers tell Gale that her daughter, a former Discovery student now getting straight As in junior secondary school, has great leadership skills, works well with others, and is looked to by fellow students to set the pace.

"They have so much confidence and positive feeling about themselves, the competition isn't a factor," adds parent Kim Reid.

Many of the staff at Discovery acted on their beliefs by enrolling their own children in the school, including Charlie Metzger, a veteran of twenty-five years' teaching experience whose three children attended Discovery. He has taught there since before his current students were born. When his children went on to secondary school, they told him the focus was no longer on getting excited about learning things but on getting marks. Other former students said it was simpler to "manage the variables" in secondary school because the only significant one was the teacher—give the teacher what he or she wants and you get a good mark. That's why Metzger feels Discovery produces "more well-rounded, complete kids who can deal with the exigencies of life."

The exercise his two dozen students were working on during my visit revolved around Europe. They learned math by using chalk on the carpeted floor to sketch a grid representing lines of longitude and latitude. They learned geography by overlaying the grid with a classroom-sized map of the continent, using hundreds of inch-long wooden rods. Later, they would take the school on a "tour" of Europe to explain what they've learned in social studies and language.

TYNEHEAD MONTESSORI

A third Surrey district school offering yet another approach to teaching is Tynehead Montessori School. It's part of a worldwide teaching movement based on the principles espoused by turn-of-the-century Italian educator Maria Montessori, who professed the need to make the abstract concrete for children. For instance, children learn multiplication by manipulating objects that represent numbers. Although the instruction style is less teacher-centred than child-centred and uses teacher- and student-created materials rather than textbooks, Montessori education places a strong emphasis on phonics, grammar, math, and history. However, the students at Tynehead don't compete in sports or science fairs—since the belief is that competition should take place within the student. Social development is also considered extremely important. Kids are encouraged to take personal responsibility, do a lot of self-assessment and planning, be tolerant of other cultures, and treat people with grace and courtesy.

Principal Kerri Wallin says two distinct groups of parents send their kids to Tynehead. The first group not only believes in the Montessori method, but uses it at home. The second is made up of people "shopping" for an appropriate school who know little or nothing about Montessori. Wallin says many of these parents aren't tolerant of other cultures, and might tell their kids that a swift kick is the way to solve personal problems with others. "They're looking for a solution and they're not sure if this is it," she says.

"Sometimes [parents] think we can cure a problem child," says teacher Gloria Eyolfson. "Some children are more suited to [the Montessori method] than others."

At Tynehead, all of the teachers are specially trained in the Montessori techniques. The classes are mixed: either grades 1 to 3 or 4 to 6, and students stay with the same teacher for three years. On the day I visited, students in one grade 4-6 class were embarked on an amazing array of activities. Some were gardening, others were writing "letters to the editor" of the school newsletter, others were tending to baby rabbits, reading novels, setting up imaginary "stores" and "bank accounts" for an exercise that teaches math. It's not always so diverse: the class has a formal math period every morning, and a creative writing period each afternoon.

A framed print of Albert Einstein adorns one hallway at Tynehead. On it are his words, "Imagination is more important than knowledge."

Thomas Haney Secondary

A $20.5-million building opened in Maple Ridge in September 1992 as the joint home of a Douglas College campus and a new-concept secondary school. Thomas Haney had its genesis when Maple Ridge superintendent Denis Therrien called together a group of educators and asked them the question of a lifetime: "If you could have an ideal school, what would be the vision?" The result was a school built from the ground up based on two key principles: that students learn at different rates and different ways, and that students need to take more responsibility for their learning.

Rather than teacher-centred, lecture-style classrooms, courses at Thomas Haney are described in "learning guides," which give the information, exercises, and instructions required for each subject in sequential order. Teachers are available for one-on-one discussions, small-group seminars, and general assistance. But with learning guide in hand, a student is off to the races and is riding the horse. Twenty learning guides make one course—when the students complete them all, they're done.

The educators involved in Thomas Haney had despaired that kids failed not because they couldn't learn material but because they couldn't learn it as quickly as the rest of the class. "We all learn in different ways and at different rates. There's nothing about the traditional school that accommodates that," says principal Dave Estergard. At Haney, the theory of continuous progress is put into practice: students take tests when their teachers decide they're ready, based on their evaluation of the work the students have done in the learning guides.

To complete the vision of a school built on self-directed learning, the district hired an architect to design an appropriate building. "So many schools are being built badly. They're already confined in what they can do because they have all these cells for people to work in," says Estergard.

Thomas Haney is a beautiful building full of natural light. Its main feature is the "Great Hall of Learning." In it, kiosks are set up in various spots for students to obtain the learning guides, workbooks, and other material for their courses. There's a hum of activity there: kids working in groups of three or four, others alone at study carrels. It looks more like a university library than a secondary school. Off to the side are some classrooms where teachers offer scheduled seminars.

There is no timetable per se at Haney. It's up to each student to spend time planning his or her weekly and daily schedule. For each course, they are assigned one teacher as a "marker" but they can choose any teacher for help, subject to the schedules that teachers post. (As a result, no student can complain they're doing poorly because his or her teacher dislikes them.) Once the marker says they're ready to take a test, it's up to the students to schedule an appointment at the testing centre, where a staff member hands out the tests and supervises.

For each student, a key player is the teacher advisor (or TA). Similar to the idea expressed in the Royal Commission, each staff member in the school is mentor to eighteen or nineteen students in a mix of grades. The students have the same teacher advisor for as long as they stay in the school, which gives the personal contact that's helpful in any big secondary school and essential at a self-directed one. In addition, the TA keeps an eye on the students' schedules and consults with their subject teachers if there are any problems.

"The opportunity for kids to work with adults on a one-to-one basis is very powerful," says Estergard. "The kind of relationship between a teacher and a kid here is quite different. You become an adult supporter and aide, versus a somewhat more authoritarian relationship."

The first year of existence for Haney was by no means smooth.

Hell on wheels would be a better description, according to Estergard's explanation of events. The school was ready for occupancy only five days before classes began; ordered texts didn't arrive on time; a lot of other schools sent "their renegades" to the new school; the staff was five teachers short the first month because of higher-than-projected registration; the computer software for recording student progress on the learning guides was poor; the learning guides themselves "were far from perfect when we opened. They tended still to be written for teachers, not for kids." And the Maple Ridge Teachers' Association was on work-to-rule from October to April, so formal staff meetings or professional development couldn't take place. The labour dispute became a strike in April.

But the school survived partly because of the dedication of the teaching staff, who put in long hours. Like the Surrey Traditional School, the teachers at Haney chose their workplace specifically.

"It just makes total and complete sense," says humanities department head Sandy Birce when asked why she works at Haney. "I don't know how I stayed in the system as long as I did. It frustrated the hell out of me but there weren't any options."

"I've been trying to teach this way for twenty-five years," says math teacher Don Sears. He has always tried to individualize his courses for students, break texts into modules, and work one-on-one with kids. He says Haney is proving that much of the traditional lecture-style method—"stand and deliver"—is a waste of kids' time.

Sears was voted most likely to succeed at his high school, but in his first year at university, he failed two courses and passed the rest by a hair. "I was a good student. I just never woke up to the fact that you have to work. I never had to work in high school." He adds, "When [Haney students] come out of here, I hope they'll be much more self-motivated."

They also need to be self-motivated before they can graduate. "This place isn't for everybody," says French teacher Lorraine Ryan. "Not everybody can get organized enough to swim here. Some haven't learned the importance of time. They'll take off for the afternoon or wander the halls." She says Haney students need a lot of guidance because they have a lot of freedom.

Unlike other schools described in this chapter, Haney is not a choice school but draws kids from a particular catchment area in Maple Ridge. The result is some students and parents don't like its freedom. Grade 9 student Justin Olson wants Haney to be like "normal" schools. "I think we learn less because we don't have the teacher telling us what to do all day long. It's our responsibility to go to them, which I don't like really." He prefers regular classes in which "we had to sit there and listen because the teacher was talking."

Another student who isn't happy with Haney is Lee Wood. (He plans to switch to Garibaldi Secondary this fall.) "I still haven't started grade 10 French here and I'm supposed to graduate this year," he tells me during my visit. "I just need somebody to tell me what to do."

But one of Wood's friends, Kermit Thornley, says he's a better student for attending Haney. "I know how to study on my own. Before, I did no work and got As and was on the honour roll," says Thornley. "Here you learn stuff better. At a normal school you just show up and you can pass."

Others prefer Haney because it offers flexibility that traditional schools don't. "I've had so many personal problems in my life this year that at any other school, I wouldn't have been able to handle it," says grade 12 student Shelagh Nixon. She adds that lecture-style classes tend to make most kids tune out.

At Haney, says grade 10 student Cherie Jones, "You have a chance to actually make sure you understand for yourself. I find I'm actually learning things and remembering things."

The students told me it's easy to goof off at Haney even though they know they'll pay for it if they do. They also complain of line-ups to consult with teachers, and several don't like the fact that they're "behind" their classmates.

In response, teachers say goofing off and line-ups for help exist in regular classrooms, but they look different and are less visible—twenty-nine kids sitting in desks waiting on one teacher, or staring out the window daydreaming.

Staff admit that it's hard for the students to escape the conditioning of "behind" or "ahead" in courses. "Behind is a word we have to take out of our vocabulary," says Don Sears, noting that the school is fighting the notion that students must proceed in lock step and complete exactly one grade per year, as well as parents who believe it, a system that institutionalizes it and a government that practically mandates it.

Ultimately, students' success or failure at Haney depends on whether they take responsibility for their own learning. "We're prescriptive in what they learn but how they demonstrate it is often up to them," says principal Estergard. "We're pretty rigid. Kids must learn things, there's nothing airy-fairy about whether a kid learns it or not."

To students who complain that they liked it better when the teacher told them exactly what to do and how to do it, staff say, "So you want a babysitter? I find that really funny coming from a teenager." And to parents who complain that their children did better in traditional schools and blame Haney for their struggles, staff point out that if kids who can't work independently don't crash and burn in school, it will happen elsewhere, when the consequences could be greater.

"I've had parents complain that this is a correspondence school. It's only a correspondence school if their child isn't using the resource people in the proper manner," says teacher Sandy Birce.

Adds Lorraine Ryan, "If the parents don't buy into how this school works, they can't possibly instill that kind of work ethic in their kids."

LEN SHEPHERD SECONDARY (INTER-A PROGRAM)

In one hallway of this Surrey school, a team of teachers combine bits of self-directed learning, continuous progress, peer tutoring, team teaching, and integration in another popular choice program focused on preparing students for university.

Liz Gallie is the outgoing, ebullient, and confident grade 9 student assigned to be my tour guide for the Inter-A program. "I was sick of being in a system where I had no choice as to what I was going to do," says Gallie in explaining her choice of program. "I'm learning more and I'm learning better. When I go to university, I feel confident I will not completely bomb."

Pedagogically, Inter-A is a bit of a hodgepodge. In the sciences and the humanities, students progress at the speed of the class, but they take math at their own pace. Three years of math are divided into eighteen "packages," similar to the learning guides of Thomas Haney. The system has reduced the three-year math program by one-third by eliminating review material: teachers say students retain math better in Inter-A than they would in other schools.

Almost all the work in Inter-A is done in groups. That teaches students how to deal with interpersonal problems and allows for peer tutoring, for which students receive extra marks. But one problem in doing group work is the physical set-up: the program is crammed into too little space in a number of separated classrooms.

The seed for the program was planted when English teacher Vic Vollrath and social studies teacher John Harper pulled back the folding door that divided their rooms and created humanities classes. From there, they branched out to include math and physical education, all within the constraints of the regular school timetable. Eventually, as other teachers joined the team, it coalesced into a separate program for grades 8 to 10. It was popular and successful enough that parents asked the school to extend it to grades 11 and 12 and now there's a demand for grade 7 (partly because parents of Montessori-educated students are looking for somewhere for their kids after that program ends in grade 6).

The morning I visited, students and teachers were preparing for evening interviews with prospective students. Teacher Rick Soon tells the student interviewers to ask themselves whether the would-be students are applying to Inter-A because they want to be there or because they're being forced to.

"It works for any student who wants to be here, wants to learn, and is willing to put in the time and effort," says Soon. "Kids who are here to play, who aren't concerned about their work, or who don't have parents who are concerned about their work, they'll struggle."

Soon says he likes the flexibility of the timetable for taking students on in-depth field trips and thinks the program teaches kids how to learn better than traditional schools. "They're better prepared for the university-type courses where there's a lot of independent work done."

Adds Liz Gallie, "You have to be self-motivated. No one's going to be chasing you around and telling you what to do."

LANGLEY FINE ARTS SCHOOL

The only public visual and performing arts school in B.C.—and one of only two in Canada west of Toronto—is in the tiny village of Fort Langley near the banks of the Fraser River. Another choice school, kids attend from all over the Langley district as well as significant numbers from Surrey and Coquitlam. It's unique not only for its arts orientation but its student body—grade 1 through grade 12.

It tends to be that attending the school is the parents' decision for kids up to grade 7, then the students make the choice after that. Not all of the elementary kids continue on to the secondary grades, and many of the students attending secondary school there did not start out in the elementary school. Like other choice schools, parents play an important role, but parents of secondary students aren't always as involved. "There are kids here on welfare and there are kids whose mom and dad drop them off in the morning in the Mercedes," says principal Peter Beckett.

Introducing himself to a group of prospective students and their parents during an open house, he begins, "I'm the principal of the Langley Fine Arts School and I thoroughly enjoy coming to work each day." Beckett explains that the arts and academics are "equal partners" at the school. "We think the arts can do some pretty significant things for kids. We're not here to create future artists."

Students are exposed to all the fine arts (drama, music, dance, and visual arts) until grade 7. At grade 8 they choose two of the four areas in which to concentrate for five hours each per week and in grade 9 they pick only one and receive seven hours of instruction in it weekly. To accommodate the extra time devoted to the arts, academic courses are structured on the semester system and taught in less time than in other schools.

Vice-principal Terrie Levitt warns that Langley Fine Arts is not an easy ride because students need a sense of self-discipline. "If they don't have organizational skills or don't stay on top of their homework, they can drown here," she says.

Beckett adds that some students are surprised to discover that the arts courses feature structured assignments. "You're not just going to be turned loose with a paintbrush."

In most schools, art and drama are notorious catch-alls for students who are discipline problems, but at Langley Fine Arts, class clowns aren't welcomed even by the students. Particularly at the secondary level, they're a serious, committed, even driven bunch.

The student body is not all kids with nose rings. It is mostly white, but within that, there are students who participate in a lunch-time Bible-study club and some who are openly gay, lesbian, or bisexual. "The range of tolerance here is the antithesis of the fundamental schools," says Beckett.

The students who choose Langley Fine Arts make some sacrifices. There are no school sports teams. Classes start as early as 7:30 a.m. and run as late as 4:30 p.m. Some upper-level academic options attract little interest so students who need them for university take them by correspondence.

The school was not built for the arts and is also stuck with its share of portable classrooms. For instance, the drama room is a converted woodworking shop. But it's getting a $4.2-million addition: two dance studios and art rooms, an art gallery, drama room, and new library, as well as a second phase of secondary classrooms and lab space.

Beckett feels schools like Langley Fine Arts that have their own special environment and sense of community are the way of the future. "There's a culture in this school. It is focused, it has a more common sense of purpose and discussion," he says. "The animal that's dying is the local neighbourhood comprehensive school. The concept that the local neighbourhood school can be all those things to all people in a neighbourhood is inappropriate and untenable.

In the process of trying to do everything, it finds out it can't and ends up doing a little bit less for everybody."

This small sample of schools suggests there's a variety of programs available in the B.C. education system; there are many teachers passionately committed to their profession; parents are welcome to get involved. But the main point of these six school visits is to show some of the different visions of the school system. That's an issue that's fundamental to the debate over Year 2000, yet often wasn't articulated in the public discourse. It's more than a question of what is the purpose of schooling. That's something on which even a diverse and pluralistic society such as ours can reach some sort of agreement. The tougher question is: How do we achieve that purpose? This chapter explored some different pedagogical approaches. The next chapter will explore the differing ideological ideas, a discussion that offers no easy answers.

[9]
POLITICS AND THE NEXT
EDUCATION ISSUES

During the 1994-95 school year, demands for a "traditional" school modelled on the Surrey version spread to at least a dozen other districts: among them Duncan, Abbotsford, Burnaby, North Vancouver, Peace River North, Parksville-Qualicum, Maple Ridge, Comox, Squamish, and Delta. The proposals have met with mixed response from school boards—Abbotsford opened a traditional school in the fall of 1995, some boards have supported the proposals in principle, and others have rejected them, including the North Vancouver board.

One of the reasons the North Vancouver plan was turned down was cost, explains superintendent Robin Brayne. The proposal declared that "no further operating costs per pupil will accrue to the district" but that was patently wrong. Since the proposed school would be open to kids from across the district, its pupils would likely be a handful from each school, which would not reduce the number of staff at existing schools. Some people who lobby for back-to-basics education also lobby for deficit cutting: it's hypocritical for them to make special requests asking school boards to spend more money. In addition, the district parents' council told the school board that they felt the proposal was not alternative—rather, it proposed characteristics for which all schools strive.

"A relentless focus on the instructional process, outcomes, parental involvement, exceptional teaching should happen in all schools," says Brayne. Starting a school from the ground up with school uniforms, a structured environment, direct instruction, and a covenant signed by parents is not the only way to boost educational achievement.

So what are the best ways of educating kids for the highest possible outcomes for all? Can the style of education proposed in traditionsal schools really meet the demands of the 21st century or is it in fact a step backwards? David Robitaille of UBC likens the back-to-basics vogue with people's reaction to letting kids use calculators. Parents recalled how much time and work it took them to do long division and they wondered, "What kind of generation will we raise if they don't know how to do all that boring stuff we learned?" Somehow, tedious was equated with good for you, like eating your educational spinach—no pain, no gain, if you enjoy it, you can't be learning. This mind-set yearns for the familiar, and the norm for the school system has been dull.

"My question to people is always, 'Well, how much did you like school?'" says trustee Jackie Tegart. Usually the answer is "Not very much," yet Tegart finds that many people's main criticism of the school system is that kids enjoy school too much, they're having too much fun. "What else should we do if we want lifelong learners?" asks Tegart.

"With the advent of technology, they need problem-solving skills and critical-thinking skills and you don't get that from a teacher lecturing, from sitting in rows and wearing uniforms," says UBC dean of education Nancy Sheehan. She says we'll hurt "a whole generation" if we embrace the traditional model.

"Too much control on the part of teachers, too much lecturing, not enough ownership on the part of students" are the *problems* with teaching, not the solutions, says SFU education professor Marv Wideen. And a growing emphasis on standardized outside testing is not going to make the schools better places because the only thing students will learn is how to figure out what they need to memorize. "That's the education for a new society?" asks Wideen.

"We kill too many intellects with the emphasis on traditional skills. Education should enrich your life so that you wouldn't want to do anything else," says Maurice Gibbons, a professor emeritus at SFU whose research focused on self-directed learning. He says the focus on content inherent in traditional schools makes control by the teacher endemic: the teacher controls what is learned, how it's learned, and how long it takes, leaving no power to the student. And with no power, students consider their schooling boring and irrelevant. To keep students from dropping out due to boredom, Gibbons argues that we need powerful ways of learning-through-experience: teaching that exercises the intellects of young people, rather than stuffing them with facts. "We aren't in training to do well on 'Jeopardy'," says Gibbons. "This move backward may be the demise of schooling as we know it. I don't think the traditional model of schooling can prepare kids for the future. We need some radical changes."

Gibbons says the traditional model has been outstripped by technology. It used to be that only the teacher could provide students with "information"—now that's available by tapping on computer keyboards. Consequently, the teacher's role should shift toward inspiring, guiding, and helping students, teaching them how to set goals, find out information for themselves, and process that information.

People who call for a return to the old days have "some fantasy in their head as to what was going on in school back in the fifties, that somehow we were graduating 100 percent of students and they all got high marks and all of them were good citizens and it all came about because they sat in rows and had lectures. It's a fantasy," declares Education Minister Art Charbonneau. He points out that schools today are home to kids from a wider range of backgrounds, while in the good old days nearly half the population left school by grade 10. The rest had an academic bent and came disproportionately from middle-class families. "We had far fewer problems in society at large. We did not have the substance abuse problems, the drug abuse problems, we didn't have the sort of family fracture, or alternate families, you name it. We didn't have kids worrying in the fifties about AIDS and a dozen other things. Those are the problems that walk in the door of our school. All of society's problems come into the school. . . . Going back to a mythological classroom where they all come in neatly dressed, have their hair short and combed, and they're going to now learn, it's a fantasy."

None of this is to say that teachers should completely abandon direct instruction. Such either-or dichotomy causes nothing but polarization. But these arguments certainly imply the need for less emphasis on direct instruction. Why do people want to send their kids to schools that hold direct instruction above all other models? The parental push for traditional schools is about more than teaching techniques, although that's the way it's presented to school boards.

It's about values and politics. Most of the parents who want to send their kids to these schools will freely acknowledge that they believe in the importance of certain conservative morals. Like any parent, they want to send their children to a school where social problems and violence don't exist. No one can be criticized for that sentiment. But probe deeper, and you'll see that they want to send their children to a school where the other children come from homes where the same values and morals are espoused. They want their kids to be with the children of other like-minded parents, people who share the same religious, ideological, or political philosophies.

SECONDARY SCHOOLS

Art Charbonneau claims that most teachers have moved away from the direct-instruction, lecture-style presentation, but at the secondary-school level, that's not true. On average, the typical method of instruction in Canadian secondary schools is stand-and-deliver, lectures by the teacher, with the teacher controlling the pace and doing 80 percent of the talking. Student participation tends to amount to repetition of what teachers say or answering teachers' questions. Variety in a social studies class can mean that one day students copy notes from a board, the next day it's from the overhead, and the third day they read through the textbook and make notes. In other words, cries for a traditional school as an alternate program are misguided—traditional is the status quo.

"If you say, 'This is a traditional school,' it assumes that schools are now otherwise, somehow entirely nontraditional. It's really not the case," says Royal Commission researcher Valerie Overgaard.

The ubiquity of direct instruction in the higher grades is one of the reasons why secondary schools are the next frontier in education change in B.C. When I argue that Year 2000 is alive, I'm only talking about the elementary schools. In secondary schools, it's like a premature baby in critical condition, clinging to life intravenously.

Even former education minister Anita Hagen is willing to admit the need for reform in secondary schools is key. "The secondary schools have been the same since I started to teach in a secondary school, and although there were many many good things happening, the kind of impetus for change, the recognition of a changing society and changing economy hasn't filtered through."

"I take seriously what the Royal Commission had to say about grade 11 and 12, that it is not a program that serves the needs of the majority of students who are in school," says Milt McClaren of

SFU. "That statement is as true today as it was when the Royal Commission wrote it. And in spite of Skills Now, which is an attempt to address that challenge, in spite of work experience, in spite of regulation changes to the graduation program, I still believe basically the conditions that exist in the high schools are the same as when I went to Lord Byng Secondary in 1955."

There certainly is some good teaching going on in secondary schools, but the fact remains that these institutions act as a filtering and sorting mechanism for our society. Their role is to tell universities and employers which kids should go to further education, which ones could be trained for skilled labour, which ones fit into the low-paying, dead-end service jobs.

If we want secondary schools to get beyond that, we need to solve a number of problems, educators say. The rote method of teaching is one, as discussed. The rate of progress—with everyone in the class moving at the same pace, even if they could go faster or need to go slower—is another. And the number of teachers students face—and the number of students per teacher—make schools more like assembly lines or factories: efficient, but dehumanizing. "I've never met anybody who said secondary schools are good structures for people," says Charles Ungerleider of UBC.

Secondary schools must resolve two competing tensions, says Dave Watkins, the graduation program team leader. On one hand, he sees the need to personalize education and make it relevant to each individual; on the other hand is the need to create cohesion and identity in a school. He predicts that schools will respond to the future by inventing a diverse variety of answers.

These changes can't come quickly or easily, but the government has made some initial steps, in particular with the Career and Personal Planning program. And schools themselves are bringing about reforms by trying to break away from the five-by-eight timetable (in which students rotate through five of their eight subjects per day in sequence). Timetable reform has some potential to enhance both student-teacher contact and continuous progress.

One timetable that's being explored is the "Copernican" version (also known as the horizontal timetable or the quarter system) in which students take only two subjects at a time—one in the morning and one in the afternoon, and switch to another two after ten weeks, dividing the year into quarters. The philosophy is that students will learn material better by taking it in intensive doses and by not having so many different courses vying for their attention. The Copernican timetable was pioneered in B.C. in 1991-92 by

L.V. Rogers Secondary in Nelson and was credited for big drops in course failure rates and big jumps in provincial exam scores. Since then, the timetable has been adopted by twenty-six other secondary schools including Johnston Heights in Surrey and Sa-Hali Junior Secondary in Kamloops. Schools that embark on the timetable find common bugs that need to be worked out—teacher preparation time, the need for daily band practice and physical education, what to do about students who transfer to or from schools on different timetables, students loaded with two heavy subjects in one quarter and two light subjects in another, and how much material will be retained if a student takes a subject in the first quarter of one year then doesn't have it again until the final quarter of the next year. But the schools that have adopted it say the benefits—which also include spin-offs such as better attendance and more personal contact between teachers and students—outweigh the difficulties.

Some secondary schools are altering their timetables to accommodate the newly required two-credit courses in fine arts and practical arts. Templeton Secondary in East Vancouver anticipated the changes and switched in September 1994 to a four-block-per-day schedule, what might be called the "two-by-four" timetable. It means that classes are slightly longer, causing concern about the attention span of students, but its benefits are several, says principal Lorne Kerr. Students face one of only two different teachers in the first block of every day, so their attendance can be monitored more closely; back-to-back blocks can be scheduled for all-morning or all-afternoon field trips; students never have the same class two days in a row, so homework can be more evenly distributed. Even the longer classes have proved beneficial. "When you have more time, you have to move toward a different teaching style," says Kerr. "You can't talk for eighty minutes, so you do more co-operative learning and discussion groups." Templeton was the first Vancouver school to switch to this timetable, but it was following in the footsteps of schools in Burnaby.

Former ministry veteran Jack Fleming is happy to see schools trying to make scheduling more flexible because five years ago, the five-by-eight timetable was seen as sacrosanct. "In most secondary schools, you'll find some teachers already working out informal ways to get around the timetable, get around the strict subject regimentation, get around the specific traditions that are so built into what they do."

Another idea for change is the middle-school concept. Far from a radical switch, it's just a restructuring of the grades within buildings—creating a set of schools that house kids from grades 6 to 8. In New Brunswick, junior high school is grades 7 to 9 and high school grades 10 to 12, and they've been that way for generations. The idea is to offer kids a more gradual transition to secondary school during the difficult period of early adolescence. Coquitlam and West Vancouver are among the districts experimenting with middle schools.

Making schools smaller is another idea that some propose. However, it's of limited utility. For one thing, half of the secondary schools in the province already are small, with fewer than 300 kids, and they wish they could be bigger so they could offer a wider choice of programs, so smaller is not necessarily better. And then there's the cost factor. "In a perfect world, perhaps we wouldn't have schools of larger than 500 or so," says Art Charbonneau. "However, to build a high school for 500 students with all of the lab facilities and shops and all of the athletic facilities, it's impossible. If you're talking about Surrey or Richmond or Vancouver or Maple Ridge, unfortunately to be economic we have to build high schools for 1,500." It's wrong to say we *must* build schools for 1,500 in the big urban centres, it's a question of political priorities: we're a free country and can choose to spend our money the way we wish, and if we knew that smaller schools were the solution, wouldn't the capital cost be worthwhile?

Building smaller schools may not be the solution, but creating smaller, friendlier environments within schools deserves a look. Charles Ungerleider of UBC offers this idea for "humanizing" education: Take eight teachers and assign them to a particular group of kids (slightly fewer than the current pupil:teacher ratio would dictate) and tell them, "You're responsible for these kids from grade 8 to 12. You know what the academic expectations are: your job is to get them there using your best professional judgement. We expect results. We want an intellectually challenging experience for all these kids. We will measure accountability. And don't lose any along the way." Working in a group with all the peer support, feedback, and pooling of skills it permits would be healthier for teachers. (Remember, secondary schools aren't only alienating for students: spending most of your workday standing in a classroom surrounded by thirty kids with no other adult colleague can be frighteningly lonely.) Obviously, this system would allow teachers to get to know kids as people and to take into account their different rates of learning. The students "are going to have a different feel about school. They'll feel they're missed because of their contribution if they don't show up," says Ungerleider. He says good teachers won't balk at the concept as long as they control how they teach.

Timetables and school structure are important, but they too are not the whole answer for the secondary grades. *What* is taught and *how* it's taught are the fundamental things. The goal is to create a school and classroom climate that gets kids engaged and involved in what they're learning, the kind of principles talked about in Year 2000.

"If all you did was ensure there was active learning in all the secondary classrooms half the time, you would have a revolution in the secondary schools," says BCTF research director Larry Kuehn. "The most fundamentally powerful thing we could have done was to try to understand what the constructivist view of education meant for secondary schools and at least ask some questions that would generate debate."

But Year 2000 was cancelled before it could really influence the secondary schools and its disappearance amounted to tacit endorsement of the status quo. The government is bringing in some changes that will help to make school more relevant for those who don't go to university and help make schools somewhat less alienating. But the biggest change—the how of teaching—is up to teachers. We'll have to wait and see what happens.

"If you were to compare the classrooms of today with ten years ago, the degree of group work and co-operative learning exercises that occur has increased dramatically," says Ken Novakowski of the BCTF. "The Year 2000 started to introduce some of those concepts and some of them have taken hold in the system."

But like any large institution, secondary schools are notoriously conservative in the "slow to change" sense of the word. Inertia is a powerful force. It's not that the people in secondary schools are necessarily resistant to change, even though some feel there's nothing seriously wrong with the system since it works for a fair number of students and teachers. Nor is the institution itself immune to change. It's just that change is difficult and the change process in British Columbia's secondary schools is far from over.

CHOICE

I've explored throughout this book the "how" of education. But as mentioned in the preceding section, the "what" is also key to meeting the needs of students. The fundamental debate that the province must wrestle with as the 21st century dawns is choice.

"How do you run a common system with common structures for a clientele as diverse as society?" asks Tom Fleming, managing as ever to capture the nub of the issue. The obvious answer is that you can't and the solution is to offer alternative structures. To an extent, they exist already in the B.C. school system. In addition to the schools we visited last chapter, there are storefront schools, French immersion programs, and a host of courses from photography to cooking. But maybe we need to refine the vision of choice even further. Recall the argument last chapter by Peter Beckett, principal of Langley Fine Arts School: a school needs an identity, a culture, a shared vision, and the comprehensive neighbourhood school trying to be all things to all people is a dinosaur.

"I don't have any difficulty with the notion of parents having the right to ask for a whole variety of schools within the spectrum," says Dickens Elementary principal George Rooney. "In fact, I would support it. I believe in schools putting forward a philosophy and living or dying by it."

It's a tempting argument that I can't really disagree with. Surveys that indicate students who drop out of school often do so because it's boring mean we're either presenting material in a boring way or else we're offering them a boring choice of material. When I visit a magnet school like Langley Fine Arts and see teenagers thrilled to be there, my immediate reaction is: "This is the answer."

Others tell me not to jump to conclusions. Kamloops superintendent Tarry Grieve says turning the public school system into a "boutique" will speed the disintegration of community. Schools are the only institutions left that can create a sense of cohesion amid the diversity of society by bringing everyone together, regardless of background. Grieve thinks schools should be "the unifying force that recognizes the individuality of people but stresses the ties that bind, not to make all of us the same but to provide a common experience."

Charles Ungerleider offers a similar argument. He says the strength of public schooling is its ability to engage people from every background in human conversation. The public school is the only thing that makes community possible, "the last meeting place" in our society. "If you segregate kids by values, you're eroding what public schools are supposed to do, which is recreate community," says Ungerleider. "Choice shouldn't be paramount as a value. The purpose of school is to extend us beyond the boundaries to which we're born. If I put my kid in a school that just explicates my values, I fail my kid."

"I have real problems with special-interest groups who want to take their children and remove them from the mainstream and deal only with those who think all the same way," says former BCSTA president Jackie Tegart. "My concern is that we lose the purpose of public schooling in this elusive chase for choice. To me, the purpose is to educate our young people in a very diverse culture and to develop understanding of others in their interactions and their problem-solving and all those kinds of things besides the intellectual development. We have to look at what kind of young people we would have coming out of our schools if we had that kind of a choice model. I'm very fearful of what would happen to our public school system in the name of choice." Tegart says the school system can offer choices and could be doing a better job at it, but that shouldn't mean segregating students.

Choice versus community. Catering to different interests versus creating a common sense of experience. A boutique of options versus a core curriculum. The choice (I use the word on purpose) is difficult. I would say it's most helpful not to think of the two philosophies in either-or terms but rather as a spectrum. It's up to us as a society to decide what balance to strike, how far to move toward emphasizing one or the other. That's still a tough decision, especially when the question of charter schools is thrown into the mix.

CHARTER SCHOOLS

Jackie Tegart's concerns about choice are noteworthy partly because they're at odds with the stance of her political party. When Tegart finished her term as BCSTA president earlier this year, she went on to seek the provincial Liberal nomination in the Yale-Lillooet riding. The Liberals' education platform released in January 1995 strongly endorsed choice schools as well as charter schools. The party is doing little to explain to the public the difference between the two and make the distinction clear.

"There needs to be some clarity around charter schools and what a choice school is," says Tegart. "I've tried very hard within the Liberal party to find out what their perception of charter schools is because a charter school has many different concepts to many different people. My concern is that a charter school offer equity of opportunity to everyone that wants to apply and that has not been the experience in the United States." She says the party has told her that equal opportunity would be part of its charter-school model, yet she still doesn't know what that would look like.

In the news release announcing its platform, the Liberal party portrayed charter schools merely as one type of choice school. "Some examples of Choice Schools include: traditional schools, home schooling, year-round schooling and charter schools, such as arts-based, science-based, technology-based and Montessori-based schools." [1] By that definition, charter schools would already exist under the name of magnet schools. That's different from what's being demanded by charter-school proponents across the border in Alberta: they want to *run* the schools. In fact, that's what charter schools are across North America—schools run independent of public school boards by groups of people who sign agreements with the provincial or state government.

So what do the Liberals mean by a charter school?

"It's not an exclusive school," Liberal leader Gordon Campbell said during an interview. "It's not a school that somehow leaves a group of people out. It's a way of giving parents an opportunity to become more fully involved in the education system. You have to maintain your standards, you have to maintain openness, opportunity for everyone in the school system to take advantage of that charter school if they want."

He says charter schools wouldn't be allowed to charge fees, restrict people from certain religious groups, neighbourhoods, or income groups. "Obviously we're not going to allow that to take place, that's not what a public school system is about," he says. "The real key about charter schools is that parents are far more actively involved."

When I ask Liberal education critic Lynn Stephens the open-ended question, "How do you define a charter school?" she replies, "A charter school would be an institution that provides a different learning environment to enhance student learning." She doesn't add its most distinguishing characteristic, that it's managed by an independent group of people, but when I mention that, she agrees.

Stephens says charter schools are more accountable than typical public schools because the parents who run them "have much more of an interest in the school. This is what people coming forward to propose a charter idea have to be very well aware of: that this does have some very serious responsibilities attached to it and is not to be taken lightly."

The Liberals don't have a firm answer to the question of whether charter schools would be bound by union contracts. "In some models that's the case, in others, it's not. I would suspect that it would be the case. I don't see any reason why the union master contract would not apply because it is a publicly funded public institution," says Stephens. I press her further: Would the Liberals if elected write into the charter school legislation that master contracts must apply? "I'm not prepared to say that at this time. That's a detail and we're not talking about details at this point in time."

The Reform party of B.C. hasn't jumped on the charter school bandwagon. "I would like to try to keep the public system as whole as possible and use charter schools primarily as a last resort," says Reform education critic Len Fox. "I don't think we want to be promoting the splitting up of the public system."

The BCTF is against charter schools, for obvious reasons. They've joined a coalition of unions and lobby groups—including the Canadian Union of Public Employees, the Canadian Federation of Students, and the B.C. Confederation of University Faculty Association—in a massive campaign in defence of public schools, criticizing charter schools as private schools with public funding. Their concern is that politicians will see charter schools and their potential for circumventing the unions as politically popular ways of saving money.

Politicians should not be promoting charter schools, says Richard Williams, a trustee representative on the intermediate steering committee. "I don't see them teaching tolerance. Political parties should use their energy to support the public system," Williams says. "It's the democratic choice to have public schools because we need to learn to get along with each other. Charter schools are going to be elite. Regular kids and poor kids are going to get left behind. If a public school is working properly, it should allow kids who don't have all the advantages—money at home, parents who care—to blossom and succeed."

Again, it's important to emphasize the difference between choice schools and charter schools. I say choice is necessary and desirable. Although Tarry Grieve and Charles Ungerleider caution earlier in this chapter against making choice paramount, I believe we need more choice in the school system, not less.

The point of a public school system is to give all children no matter who they are or where they live the same *calibre* of instruction and facilities—not necessarily the same *content*. A common core of learning through elementary school and into early secondary is necessary, but once students become teenagers and start to yearn for freedom, we can't stifle them by limiting their choices and expect them not to rebel. The more choice we give to students, the more they will feel they are in school because they're choosing to, not because they must, and the less likelihood that they will drop out. Increased choice means increased relevance and that makes for a decreased drop-out rate.

The kind of choice I'm talking about is choice of content, not choice of values; choice in secondary schools more so than choice in elementary; choice for students more than choice for parents. I'm not suggesting we allow students and parents to choose schools that would divide the population by religion or ethnicity or class or politics or values. That's what private schools are for. And we don't necessarily have to create separate magnet schools, although the argument about sense of identity by Langley Fine Arts principal Peter Beckett is persuasive. Magnet schools are nice options for heavily populated areas like the Lower Mainland, but they're a pipe dream in the north.

Charter schools are fundamentally different from choice schools. At the heart, they involve handing control over schools to people who aren't responsible to the public. The question is, Do we want elected trustees or small groups of unelected people running our schools?

One of the arguments used in favour of charter schools is the extent of parental involvement. But people who support the integrity of the public system say parents already have the chance to be highly involved in schools and they point to the choice schools such as Surrey Traditional and Discovery as perfect examples. Parent power is written into the School Act. Perhaps the reason that some parents still feel excluded from the system is that some neighbourhood schools have yet to wake up to the need for opening their doors and listening to parent advisory councils. To parents who feel genuinely frustrated with the system, I say know your rights—because you have some—and exercise them. Schools should do all they can to *encourage* parental involvement both in their children's education and in the school. There aren't a lot of things that have been proven conclusively in education research, but one that has is a strong relationship between the extent of parental involvement in a child's education and the child's performance in school.

But being *involved* in a school and *running* a school are two different things: the latter is what charter schools are about. That's one of the reasons why this currently fashionable critique of the school system actually is—once you strip away the rhetoric and the spin and get to the truth—all about politics and ideology, and therefore, power. The fact that politicians are leading the way should send warning signals to a populace that is sceptical or downright distrustful of the motives of our political leaders—government and opposition alike. Although I refuse to dismiss all Year 2000 critics as right-wing fundamentalists, the ideological connections of the back-to-basics/traditional/charter-school movement have been firmly established. It's not a conspiracy, it's simply a power struggle over schools.

THE POLITICS OF EDUCATION

Education hasn't always been a big political issue in Canada. Like so many of our trends (economic, cultural, and political), education has been an issue here at the same time as it was in the United States. For instance, the Soviet launch of the Sputnik satellite persuaded American leaders that math and science education in the U.S. was inferior to that in the U.S.S.R., so the political mood swung to that side of the spectrum. In B.C., this was manifested in the 1960 report of the Chant Royal Commission, the last before the Sullivan commission. The current back-to-basics vogue has its roots in America as far back as 1983 when the Department of Education in its report *A Nation at Risk* blamed the schools for the country's inability to compete economically with Japan. George Bush kept the momentum going with his "America 2000" plan for overhauling the school system based on the notions of *A Nation at Risk*. And in the early 1990s, charter schools became fashionable in the U.S. These issues have crept across the border and mixed with Year 2000 and the recession to create the political atmosphere of education in 1995.

It seems that politicians get more mileage out of bashing the education system than standing up for its principles, a phenomenon that stands in direct contrast to our less-than-perfect yet sacred health-care system. Where are the leaders pronouncing firmly that they will defend against attempts to "Americanize" our education or create a "two-tiered" school system?

The political parties in B.C. don't shy away from taking strong and opposing stands on education issues. The heady days of 1989 and 1990—post-Royal Commission, pre-Year 2000 controversy, when the mood was one of consensus and consultation, with the Opposition generally supporting the government's education program—are no more.

The Liberal party has done its best to ensure that education would become an election issue by throwing its support behind charter schools, and endorsing essential-service designation for schools, something that draws a sharp distinction between the Liberals and the union-friendly NDP. "I'd be glad to fight the election on whether education is an essential service or not," says leader Gordon Campbell, adding that the proposal receives widespread support during his travels around the province.

The other education platforms the Liberals put forward are politically popular: enhancing parental involvement and cutting costs through more school-based management and fewer school boards—

an idea that the NDP abandoned for fear of political backlash from communities that are part of small districts.

"A principal and their staff are just about always more capable of responding to the needs of children in a community than you will have with a monolithic ministerial bureaucracy or even in some cases a large school board," says Campbell.

"We're going to try to make sure that you [parents] feel you are a part of the system and an asset to the system as opposed to sort of an infringement or an intrusion. All of that energy and enthusiasm and support for young people should be tapped and brought into the public system," he adds.

The Liberals tend to express broad support for public education with motherhood statements. "The public school system is our opportunity to give every young person the chances that they need, the tools that they need to make their own decisions in their life," says Campbell. "We know that the job world in the next twenty-five years is all going to be oriented toward education. The more education you have, the more tools you have to take advantage of the changes that are taking place in the world, the more secure you're going to be."

But he makes an important point when he adds, "I can't remember a government that didn't say that public education was the head of the list. But the actions that show that are always pale. One of the real shifts that we have to make is not just to say it but to show it."

Jim Sherrill, associate dean of education at UBC, tells me that Gordon Campbell and an assistant met with him to hear his ideas on education. Sherrill expounded and Campbell looked interested and kept responding positively. But the assistant kept interjecting and asking, "But isn't that what the current government is doing?" And Sherrill would say, "Yes." He says he realizes that "you have to make yourself appear different in politics," but for him the bottom line is "I'm interested in what's good for the kids."

Liberal education critic Lynn Stephens, MLA for the Bible-belt riding of Langley, has one particular hobby horse about B.C. education: Learning for Living, the health- and life-skills education curriculum (since subsumed under Career and Personal Planning) that has been the target of opposition from evangelical Christian groups. Stephens brought this up in my interview with her without any prompting, telling me that many people have "concerns" about issues discussed and material used in Learning for Living/Career and Personal Planning.

"There are lots of people who wonder whether what is being taught should be taught in the schools," says Stephens. "Children need to know life skills. Now the question is what life skills? Who's teaching them? How is it being taught? There are a lot of parents who believe that responsibility is theirs to a large degree."

She continues, "I'm still uncomfortable with aspects of the Learning for Living curriculum. I'm still uncomfortable with the teachers' knowledge of what they're teaching or the lack of knowledge of what they're teaching."

But she refuses to say exactly what content in the curriculum bothers her. "Many people have these concerns and I share some of those concerns," says Stephens. So I ask her if she wants to tell me what specific concerns she shares. "No I don't. Not at this time." And when I ask her what the Liberal party will do about Learning for Living if elected, she says a decision has been made but she won't reveal it. "It's not that we haven't discussed it, it is not for broad distribution."

Stephens isn't too sure how Learning for Living and Year 2000 are connected, but she knows she doesn't like either. "What flowed from the Year 2000 was the Learning for Living curriculum. And the Learning for Living curriculum that was begun in the primary has now been extended to the intermediate and the grad level." She says the philosophy of "no competition, no marking" defines Year 2000 and adds, "The Learning for Living is the curriculum that embodies that philosophy."

In the Legislature, she looked at it differently. "As for the personal and career planning features, probably the biggest objections—among people that I speak to anyway—are in the area of the 'Learning for Living' curriculum, which seems to be the basis of much, if not most of Year 2000 philosophy and the intermediate and graduation programs." [2]

Which came first, the chicken or the egg?

Stephens gave the Legislature a few more hints than she gave me about her problems with Learning for Living. She said a criticism of the program "is that it deals with the social, emotional and spiritual dimensions of development . . . attitudes, feelings, values, morals and ethics." [3]

Meanwhile, the Reform party had yet to develop its education platform when I finished writing this book in early June. Its MLAs are former members of the Social Credit party, but there's no endorsement of the Socred education platform that became known as Year 2000. Len Fox, one of only six Socreds elected in 1991, quickly points out that even then, the party "ran split" on Year 2000 and he didn't support it. "There was the hierarchy within the party that felt ownership and pushed those values but I did not," says Fox, noting his firm belief in competition. "Anything that had to do with competition was removed from the Year 2000," he says. "We have to bring that competitiveness back into the system."

In broad terms, Reform endorses cost-cutting measures in education. Fox says policy objectives can be set at the district level, but the ability to manage should be given to principals. And rather than coming from the ranks of the best teachers, administrators should be people with specific management skills.

"If we don't do that the school system as we see today will not be retained. We'll see a breakup of the public school system," says Fox. "We're going to have to do away with district bureaucracy and put more responsibility on school administrators so that they in fact have more autonomy in the running of their school. Subsequently, you're going to have to have principals that have some academic training around the running of a corporation, a plant, and the responsibilities and the talents that go with that."

Fox says where the education system has gone wrong is putting too many social responsibilities on schools. "You used to go to school to learn the three Rs. Now you go to the schools to learn how to wash your hands, how to look after yourself, almost how to dress because you're not getting that guidance at home," he says. "The teacher today almost has to be a psychiatrist, a doctor, the last thing they have to be is a teacher."

After reading the many thoughtful things people have said about education in this book, if you take the comments of Campbell, Stephens, and Fox and add them together with Mike Harcourt's "failed the grade" announcement about Year 2000, you'll come to the conclusion that what politicians of all stripes have to say about education is remarkably shallow, if not downright misleading. The politics of style over substance, rhetoric over reason, fudging over facts is playing at a school near you. "Education politics is like a western: people want to see blood in the streets, or else they'll be disappointed," says Tom Fleming.

Politicizing the schools lowers the quality of instruction and limits the ability of teachers to teach, says SFU professor Marv Wideen. "Leave the schools alone and let the teachers teach. Just support the teachers in the schools to do innovative things. Get rid of the school fixers and the bureaucrats. I wouldn't have said that five years ago, but now I could support that notion."

Although people in the education system loathed the confrontational nature of the 1980s under Social Credit, they haven't been thrilled with the NDP either, for more than just its stance on Year

2000. By targeting a larger and larger portion of its funding to school districts, the government has given school boards less discretion on spending money. Even though the government says it supports the concept of decentralizing decision-making, targeted funds have made for greater centralized control of policy. And now the fear is that around election time, politicians will do things to gain political points.

Yet if the Liberals or Reform win the provincial election, "Heaven help us," says Wideen. "It's the only reason I'll support the NDP. Harcourt leaped upon the right-wing agenda because he's a clever politician. He saw it as a way of striking some votes and getting some votes. I don't suspect the NDP really believed the right-wing agenda, but they'll borrow it if it means getting elected. The problem with the Liberals and the Reform party is they believe it."

"Given the lust for slashing the budgets at the neglect of everything else, there will be all sorts of interest in privatizing education, decentralizing and farming it out. That can be helpful but there's a point at which you undermine public education," says Wideen's colleague Roland Case. He's concerned it will further erode confidence in the school system and cause it to splinter.

More fundamentally, people are concerned about the effect of change in government on the stability of the education system. Will more changes be foisted upon the schools? Will the next set of reforms throw the good of Year 2000 out with the bad?

Kids are in jeopardy in an unstable system, because outside forces have an effect on the classroom in such ways as staff morale and cynicism about reform proposals, says Kamloops superintendent Tarry Grieve.

"Stability really describes what a lot of people crave, they absolutely crave it," says Ken Novakowski of the BCTF. "Teachers want to teach and there's an awful lot of frustration with education being a political football, but it is a public system. I don't think there's any escaping it because it needs to be responsive to what the public in the broadest sense wants to see happening in its schools. The only time that [instability] will change is when the public mood directs the politicians and says, 'Leave the schools alone. They're doing a good job. They're changing in their own way, they need that stability.'"

Marv Wideen proposes that what the schools need most is a period of benign neglect. "They need to be left alone to do their job. They're not being left alone. They're being harassed, they're being pushed, they're being prodded, cajoled, they're being insulted. With each successive generation of politicians and policy makers, they're having to face another barrage of insults."

Benign neglect probably sounds like a good idea to many. The schools have been through so much since the Royal Commission, which was supposed to calm things down after times that were even more turbulent. The system would be hard pressed to cope with another period of turmoil. And less interference would allow the best vestiges of the Year 2000 to be nurtured and take hold in the system.

But none of this is to say that education should remain outside the realm of or be above politics. To say that schools are not political is to be naive. The kind of school system we create is an expression of our political nature. Ultimately, education is a political and ideological statement about how we want children to be. School is a very potent context for perpetuating values, so it makes sense that parties want to realize their values by shaping the education system. That's what democracy is all about.

In fact, politics is *inherent* in everything to do with education and people who care about the school system have to be aware of that fact. They must always be prepared to question the motives of political leaders and decision-makers.

Education battles—whether during or between elections—must be fought on substantive issues, not slogans and sound bites and controversy. Many people credit the Year 2000 for opening up a public debate about education reform. I agree, but argue further that although a debate took place, it unfortunately didn't get beyond a shallow level in the public sphere. Despite the complexity of education and the importance with which people imbue it, most people's knowledge of the school system is surface. (Witness all the polls that showed how little people knew about Year 2000 even though it was being called the biggest school reform process in Canadian history.) The truth about what goes on behind the walls of our schools remains a mystery to most. And it's made especially tough for average people when they have to sort through all the politicking that goes on about school these days.

Where politics gets in the way is when political partisanship takes precedence over reality. In an article called "Good Education, Bad Politics", Wisconsin educator Michael Hartoonian says politics is a big reason why school reforms usually emphasize "information" (facts and figures) over "knowledge" (skills and understanding) even though knowledge is more important and relevant for students and society. "We hold to information because emphasizing knowledge would demand a *political honesty* that politicians could not explain in a 30-second news clip." [4]

Or, as author Heather-jane Robertson said at a conference in March 1995, "Our children have every right to expect more from us than what is politically expedient." [5]

The short-term view of politics may not fit with the long-term best interests of school kids and society. Politicians face an election at least every five years: it takes much longer to see benefits from education reforms.

But it is possible to get beyond political self-interest in making decisions about education. What governments need to do is foster frank, open, and honest discussion on the goals of school and the means of achieving them. The discussion must include respect for what all parties bring to the table, but the parties must put forward their perspective of what's best for *kids*, not what's best for themselves. Conflict and differences of opinion are fine, so long as the debate is based on reality and not misinformation or political rhetoric. Unfortunately, those two factors were the source of much of what has happened to Year 2000.

1. "BC Liberals Say Choice is Essential For Educational Excellence," news release, B.C. Liberal Party, January 19, 1995.

2. Debates of the B.C. Legislature, June 13, 1994, p. 11836.

3. Ibid., p. 11837.

4. Hartoonian, Michael, "Good Education, Bad Politics: Practices and Principles of Reform," *Education Digest*, November 1991, p. 33. Emphasis in original.

5. Speech at "In the Public Interest," a BCTF conference on public education, March 4, 1995, Vancouver.

Conclusion

As this book is published, students are heading back to class for the 1995-96 school year and a new set of reforms is taking effect: the changes to the intermediate and graduation programs as laid out in the government's K-12 education plan, along with new versions of curriculum for the elementary years. It should make for an interesting autumn: people are expecting implementation problems with the curricula because they've only had them in their hands since April. And remnants of cynicism continue to make some in the system distrust the government's promises of reform because they've seen so many proposals come and go.

It's been seven years since the Sullivan Royal Commission. The kids that entered kindergarten a month after the report was issued are now more than halfway through their public education. What have we done for them through these years of on-again, off-again reforms?

The education community in B.C. knows a lot more now about how kids learn than it did before the commission. "I don't know any other jurisdiction that's got the philosophical underpinnings and a clearer understanding of what needs to be done to improve the nature of schooling than this province does," says Jack Fleming.

"Those three learning principles are emerging as . . . the best thing that anybody's ever done. Educators have had it brought to their mind forcefully enough that there are some problems with the way they do things."

Fleming says the public's view of education may not change until a generation of kids goes through a learner-focused system. "In retrospect, ten or fifteen years from now, people will look back and say, 'Yeah, something really significant did happen there.' It will be a profoundly better system for kids because it will be addressing the way that people learn. And it wasn't—and in some ways still isn't—doing that."

People in the system realize the need for change and a significant amount of change has already occurred. "For two years people made us answer the question, 'Why do we have to change?' That was one of our biggest achievements, that we killed that question," says Janet Mort. "There isn't a country in the world that is succeeding like British Columbia is with educational change even with all the turmoil and all the fuss. Countries like Australia are doing small pieces of what we're doing. There's no jurisdiction I can find that is trying to make systemic change in the entire K to 12 range. There are lots of places trying to change primary, trying to change secondary schools, dabbling in charter schools, lots of people doing pieces, but there's no other place where the attempt is systemic."

Even though the debate was rancorous, people are now willing to say it was beneficial because it switched the discourse to the substance of education rather than funding. It forced people to think about what schools should do and articulate their visions and come to grips with the need for answers. "It put education and the content of education at the forefront of people's consciousness in a way that it hadn't been before," says Charles Ungerleider.

And finally, people connected to the school system have had the chance to learn from their mistakes of implementing reforms. They realize that for reforms to take hold, as explained in Chapter 6, change must take place in the minds and hearts of teachers. "Until it does people can provide incentives, models, threats, write regulations in Victoria till they're blue in the face, insist on new procedures, all that kind of stuff, and all of that is relatively superficial," says Jack Fleming. Meanwhile, the government has been taught that it shouldn't dictate how to teach: rather, it must give people in the system time and professional development help and must acknowledge publicly that there may be hitches along the way, but that things will work out.

But there are still miles to go and some people aren't optimistic that the system can make it. "We've lost it. The capacity for the educational system to change is almost crippled," says Roland Case. "All of the promises: 'We'll be there for you. We won't let you take the flak. We'll provide the material support. We're in this for the long haul.' The flip-flop, the failure to deliver time and again."

Pessimism aside, the momentum that came with Year 2000, the excitement that was happening among educators are not completely gone. If schools have some stability for the next few years, if the partisan players stop politicizing education, if the public is willing to be informed instead of reactionary, if teachers can incorporate Year 2000 theory into practice, perhaps the result will be a big step forward in reaching the goal of "what's best for kids."

All of the questions I've raised in this book, especially the issues in the last chapter, still leave us as a society with more difficult questions than easy answers, still facing the task of struggling through the ongoing debate of what we want from our education system. Most everyone will agree that the main purpose is to teach kids how to read, write, and do math, but from there, the questions get tougher. Do we want a system that makes its products obedient and polite? Anti-authoritarian and independent? Open-minded? Critical? Good at memorizing facts? Able to quote Shakespeare? Artistic? Practical? And even if we can agree on what the goals are, we're left with the struggle of how much emphasis to put on each and, ultimately, how to accomplish them. It's not an exact science: rather, these are political, ideological questions to be answered.

This is a call for co-operation in trying to find the answers. Teachers need to be more flexible in dealing with the uniqueness of each child. Unions need to consider the best interests of kids, not just their members. Politicians need to show courage and vision and stand up for public education, not just for what's popular. Bureaucrats must be willing to allow more humanity into the system. Each parent must remember that although his or her child is important, the school system is there for the benefit of all. And we as a society must examine what we're asking when we demand something from the schools to ensure our demands don't get in the way of what's best for kids.

The public has responsibilities. Seek out information. Understand the issues. Vote in school board elections. And always, the key thing we must be wary of is dishonesty. We must be vigilant for the truth about education and not buy into myths about illiteracy and failing schools, or on the contrary, the excellent quality of every teacher and the benevolence of the unions. Always ask: What is this person's or group's self-interest? First of all, remember the amount of money involved—$4 billion a year in B.C. alone. Where there's money to be spent, power politics are inherent because everyone wants a piece of the pie. Beware of politicians who try to get votes by complaining about the quality of education in the school system and claiming that they will make it shape up. Beware of critics with simplistic convictions and even more simplistic solutions. Beware of people who promote their own attempts to get power over our schools as "choice."

The school system is not perfect, nor is it in crisis. The truth, as usual, lies somewhere between the two extremes: the schools could do with some improvement. The solution is not just choice or more flexible timetables or better pupil-teacher contact or active learning or better quality instruction or parent involvement or continuous progress or self-esteem or school meals or better professional development or less political interference or less reactionary criticism or better-written report cards. It's all of them, and then some.

Schooling is a complex business, and the issues discussed in the last chapter and the rest of this book will require complex solutions. I refuse to offer any simple ones. All I will say is that when we try to find the solutions, we make sure the discussion is based on reality, not misconceptions. Only then can we disarm the bullies who try to mess with the education system based on their prejudices.

SOURCES

Chapter 1

BCTF violence survey:

Malcolmson, John D. "Teaching in the '90s: Teacher perceptions of violence in B.C. schools." Vancouver: B.C. Teachers' Federation research department, 1994.

The political climate of Canadian education in the early 1990s:

Barlow, Maude and Heather-Jane Robertson. *Class Warfare: The Assault on Canada's Schools.* Toronto: Key Porter, 1994.
Contenta, Sandro. *Rituals of Failure: What Schools Really Teach.* Toronto: Between the Lines, 1993.
Fleming, Thomas. "Canadian school policy in Liberal and Post-Liberal Eras: Historical perspectives on the changing social context of schooling, 1846-1990." *Journal of Education Policy,* 6 (1991): 183-199.
Lewington, Jennifer and Graham Orpwood. *Overdue Assignment: Taking Responsibility for Canada's Schools.* Toronto: Wiley, 1993.
McConaghy, Tom. "Canadian Education: Voices in Conflict." *Phi Delta Kappan,* June 1994: 810-811.
Nikiforuk, Andrew. *School's Out: The Catastrophe in Public Education and What We Can Do About It.* Toronto: Macfarlane Walter and Ross, 1993.

The politics of education in B.C.:

British Columbia Ministry of Education. *Let's Talk About Schools.* Victoria: Queen's Printer, 1985.
Fleming, Thomas. "Restraint, Reform and Reallocation: A Brief Analysis of Government Policies on Public Schooling in British Columbia, 1981 to 1984." *Education Canada,* Spring, 1985: 4-11.
_____. "In the Imperial age and after: Patterns of British Columbia school leadership and the institution of the superintendency." *B.C. Studies,* 81 (Spring 1989): 53-76.
_____. "Our boys in the field: school inspectors, superintendents, and the changing character of school leadership in British Columbia. In *Schools in the West.* Edited by N.M. Sheehan et al. Calgary: Detselig, 1986.
Jacobson, Elaine and Larry Kuehn. *In the Wake of Restraint: The Impact of Restraint on Education in B.C.* Vancouver: B.C. Teachers' Federation, 1986.
Kilian, Crawford. *School Wars: The Assault on B.C. Education.* Vancouver: New Star, 1985.
Tuinman, Jaap, and Robin Brayne. *The On-site Personnel who Facilitate Learning: Commissioned Papers, Volume 4.* Victoria: Queen's Printer, 1988. (See section 12)
Ungerleider, Charles S. "The Containment of Educational Conflict." *McGill Journal of Education,* 22 (1987): 131-142.
_____. "Inequality and Education: The Ideological Context of Educational Change in British Columbia." *Journal of Educational Administration and Foundation,* 2 (1987): 17-27.
_____. Power, Politics and the Professionalization of Teachers in British Columbia. In *Sociology of Education in Canada.* Edited by L. Erwin and D. Maclennan. Toronto: Kopp Clark, 1994.

Chapter 2

Documents produced by the Royal Commission on Education:

Sullivan, Barry M. *A Legacy for Learners: The Report of the Royal Commission on Education.* Victoria: Queen's Printer, 1988.
Sullivan, Barry M. *A Legacy for Learners: Summary of Findings.* Victoria: Queen's Printer, 1988.
Calam, John and Thomas Fleming. *British Columbia Schools and Society: Commissioned Papers, Volume 1.* Victoria: Queen's Printer, 1988.
Marx, Roland, and Tarrance Grieve. *The Learners of British Columbia: Commissioned Papers, Volume 2.* Victoria: Queen's Printer, 1988.

Robitaille, David F., Antoinette A. Oberg, Valerie J. Overgaard, J. Terrence McBurney. *Curriculum in the Schools of British Columbia: Commissioned Papers, Volume 3.* Victoria: Queen's Printer, 1988.
Tuinman, Jaap, and Robin Brayne. *The On-site Personnel who Facilitate Learning: Commissioned Papers, Volume 4.* Victoria: Queen's Printer, 1988.
Cutt, James, James McRae and Peter Adams. *Support Systems for Learning – Finance: Commissioned Papers, Volume 5.* Victoria: Queen's Printer, 1988.
Storey, Vernon, Elmer Froese, Arthur Kratzmann and Jack Peach. *Support Systems for Learning – Governance and Administration: Commissioned Papers, Volume 6.* Victoria: Queen's Printer, 1988.
No author. *Reports of Working Groups: Commissioned Papers, Volume 7.* Victoria: Queen's Printer, 1988.

Rationale for the Royal Commission recommendations:

Fleming, Thomas. "Understanding the Character of a 'Loose' and 'Tight' System: The Royal Commission's Recommendations and their Meaning for School Boards." Address to B.C. School Trustees Association conference, Vancouver, Jan. 26, 1989.
_____. "Prospects for Schools: The 1988 British Columbia Royal Commission on Education, Part One." *Education Canada,* Spring 1990: 11-25.
_____. "Prospects for Schools: The 1988 British Columbia Royal Commission on Education, Part Two." *Education Canada,* Summer 1990: 4-10.

Chapter 3

The study that inspired Social Credit's handling of education reform:

Decima Research and Public Affairs Communications Management. "Public Perceptions and Strategic Communications Re: Public Education in British Columbia." Unpublished document, July 30, 1988.

The government's initial response to the Royal Commission:

Brummet, Anthony J. *Policy Directions: A Response to the Sullivan Royal Commission on Education by the Government of British Columbia.* Vancouver: Ministry of Education, 1989.

BCTF paper criticizing the government's response to the Royal Commission:

B.C. Teachers' Federation. "What Really Happened to the Royal Commission Report." Unpublished document, Oct. 27, 1989.

Year 2000 framework documents:

British Columbia Ministry of Education. *Year 2000: A Curriculum and Assessment Framework for the Future (Draft).* Victoria: Ministry of Education, 1989.
_____. *Year 2000: A Framework for Learning.* Victoria: Ministry of Education, 1990.
_____. *Highlights: Year 2000 - A Framework for Learning.* Victoria: Ministry of Education, 1990

Educational philosophies and teaching methods:

Bracey, Gerald W. "Maybe not so much whole language." *Phi Delta Kappan,* November 1990: 247-248.
Dewey, John. *Democracy and Education: An introduction to the philosophy of Education.* New York: Macmillan, 1916.
Friere, Paulo. *Pedagogy of the Oppressed.* New York: Continuum, 1970.
Piaget, Jean. *The Construction of Reality in the Child.* Translated by Margaret Cook. New York: Basic, 1954.
Stahl, S.A. and P.D. Miller. "Whole language and language experience approaches for beginning reading: A quantitative research synthesis." *Review of Educational Research,* 59 (1989): 87-116.
Stahl, S.A., M.C. McKenna, and J.R. Pagnucco, "The effects

of whole-language instruction: An update and a reappraisal." *Educational Psychologist*, 29, 4 (1994): 175-185.

Vygotsky, Lev. *Thought and Language*. Edited and translated by Eugenia Hanfmann and Gertrude Vakar. Cambridge: MIT, 1962.

Walberg, H.J. et al. "What Helps Students Learn," *Educational Leadership*, 51, 4 (1994): 74-79.

Wang, M.C. and H.J..Walberg, eds. *Adapting Instruction to Individual Differences*. Berkeley: McCutchan, 1985.

Wittrock, Merlin C., ed. *Handbook of Research on Teaching* (third edition). New York: Macmillan, 1986.

Analysis of Year 2000:

British Columbia Ministry of Education. *Year 2000 Response Summary*, Victoria: Ministry of Education, 1990.

Case, Roland. "Constraining school reform: Troubling Lessons from British Columbia." Paper presented at the Restructuring Education Conference, Ontario Institute for Studies in Education, Toronto, March 5-7, 1992.

Case, Roland. "Educational Reform in British Columbia: Bold Vision/Flawed Design." *Journal of Curriculum Studies*, 24 (1992): 381-387.

Case, Roland. "Our Crude Handling of Educational Reforms: The Case of Curricular Integration." *Canadian Journal of Education*, 19 (1994): 80-93.

Flanders, Tony and Donna Wilson. *A History of the Future: Responding to the Challenges of Change*. Vancouver: B.C Teachers' Federation, 1990.

Grimmett, Peter P. "Teacher Research and British Columbia's Curricular Instructional Experiment: Implications for Educational Policy." *Journal of Education Policy*, 8 (1993): 219-239.

Hainsworth, Gavin. "The Year 2000 Referendum: Confessions of a Questioning Social Studies Teacher." *Teacher*, November/December 1992.

Hammond, David. "Two Ghosts in a House of Curriculum: Visions of the Learner and Liberal Education in Current Educational Reform." *Canadian Journal of Education*, 17 (1992): 131-147.

Hoogland, Cornelia. "Activity and the Active Learner in the Year 2000: A Deweyan Analysis." In *A Critical Analysis of British Columbia's Proposals for Educational Reform*. Edited by Roland Case. Burnaby: Simon Fraser University Faculty of Education, 1991.

Moon, Barbara J. "Getting Beyond Jargon: Constructivism in Science Education in the Year 2000." In *A Critical Analysis of British Columbia's Proposals for Educational Reform*. Edited by Roland Case. Burnaby: SFU Faculty of Education, 1991.

Overgaard, Valerie. "Learner Focused: Does it Mean What it Says or Can We Say What it Means?" In *A Critical Analysis of British Columbia's Proposals for Educational Reform*. Edited by Roland Case. Burnaby: SFU Faculty of Education, 1991.

Ungerleider, Charles S. "My Concerns About the Year 2000 Initiatives." *Teacher*, October 1992.

Wasserman, Selma. "Authentic evaluation: What Teachers Can Do." *Canadian School Executive*, November 1993, 13-21.

Werner, Walter. "Defining Curriculum Policy Through Slogans." *Journal of Education Policy*, 6 (1991): 225-238.

Chapter 4

Primary, intermediate and graduation program proposals:

British Columbia Ministry of Education. *Primary Program: Foundation Document*. Victoria: Ministry of Education, 1990.

_____. *The Intermediate Program: Learning in British Columbia (Response Draft)*. Victoria: Ministry of Education, 1990.

_____. *The Graduation Program: Response Draft*. Victoria: Ministry of Education, 1990.

Ministry-commissioned reviews of the primary program:

British Columbia Ministry of Education. *Framework for Primary Program Review*. Victoria: Ministry of Education, 1991.

_____. *Building Firm Foundations: Review of the Primary Program in British Columbia, Interim Report 1*. Victoria: Ministry of Education, 1992.

_____. *Supporting Learning: Understanding and Assessing the Progress of Children in the Primary Program*. Victoria: Queen's Printer, 1992.

Horizon Research and Evaluation. *Primary Program Review: School Research Groups*. Prepared for the B.C. Ministry of Education, June 1994.

Leithwood, Kenneth and Byron Dart. *Building Commitment for Change and Fostering Organizational Learning: Final Report for Phase Four of the Research Project "Implementing British Columbia's Education Policy"*. Prepared for the B.C. Ministry of Education, December 1993.

_____. *Building Commitment for Change: A Focus on School Leadership (Final Report for Year Two of the Research Project Implementing the Primary Program)*. Prepared for the B.C. Ministry of Education, 1991.

O'Henly, Adrienne. *Primary Program Review: Highlights from university and college reports on initiatives undertaken to support the primary program*. Prepared for the B.C. Ministry of Education Research and Evaluation Branch, July 1993.

Ross, Nell. *Primary Program Review: Education partner initiaitves in support of implementation*. Prepared for the B.C. Ministry of Education, December 1993.

Toutant, A. *Findings from the Primary Program Institute: Reflections and Directions*. Prepared for the B.C. Ministry of Education, May 17. 1993.

Zellinsky, Pat. *Primary Program Review: 1993 Survey of teachers pilot study, report of survey responses*. Prepared for the B.C. Ministry of Education, August 1993.

Analysis of the primary program:

Gammage, Philip. "Changing Ideologies and Provision in Western Canadian Primary Education." *Comparative Education*, 27 (1991): 311-321.

Hilborn, Kay. "Looking at Learning: Facing a Paradigm Shift." *Research Forum*, Spring 1990: 35-37.

Johns, Carol. "The Primary Program: What's Myth? What's Fact?" *Teacher*, November/December 1992.

McLaughlin, Patti. "Understanding 2000." *Teacher*, May/June 1990.

Various authors. *Prime Areas*, Fall 1990. Special issue on the primary program. See especially articles by Betty Boult, Ramona Langton, Marianne McTavish, Lynn Popoff, Judith Preen, Pamela Proctor.

Analysis of the intermediate program:

Chapman, Anita. "The Intermediate Program: What's Myth, What's Fact?" *Teacher*, October 1992.

Lewis, Cynthia. "Principles of Curricular Integration for Informed Implementation." In *A Critical Analysis of British Columbia's Proposals for Educational Reform*. Edited by Roland Case. Burnaby: SFU Faculty of Education, 1991.

Toutant, Arnold. *Field Response to the Intermediate Program: Summary Report*. Queen's Printer, Victoria, 1992.

Analysis of the graduation program:

Fleming, Thomas, Anne Davies, Cynthia Chambers, and Robin Brayne. *A Colloquium on the Year 2000 and the draft Graduation Program: The Secretariat's summary of discussions among school, college, university and business representatives*. A report to the B.C. Ministry of Education and to colloquium participants, Victoria, 1991.

Flick, J. et al. "Year 2000: Faculty of Arts Report." Unpublished document submitted to UBC committee on Year 2000, November, 1990.

Sherrill, James. "The Man From Grad." *UBC Education*, Winter 1993.

Slaymaker, Olav. "Educational reform in B.C.: The challenge of multiculturalism, competitiveness and sustainability in the 21st century." Paper presented at workshop Education for the 21st century, Richmond, B.C., Nov. 13, 1993.

Thomson, Kathleen. "McEducation in the New Age: The Future and the Year 2000." In *A Critical Analysis of British Columbia's Proposals for Educational Reform*. Edited by Roland Case. Burnaby: SFU Faculty of Education, 1991.

Cabinet review of Year 2000:

Hagen, Stanley B. *Education Reform in British Columbia: Building a Sustainable School System*. Victoria: Ministry of Education, September 1991.

The NDP platform on Year 2000:

No author. "The New Democratic Party of B.C. talks to School Trustees about the Ministry of Education's Year 2000 blueprint for education." Unpublished document, December 1989.

Chapter 5

Anita Hagen's tenure as Education Minister:

Kuehn, Larry. "Schooling Under the NDP: The British Columbia Experience." *Our Schools/Our Selves*, October/November, 1993: 27-44.

Further drafts of the intermediate and graduation programs:

British Columbia Ministry of Education. *The Intermediate Program: Foundations*. Victoria: Ministry of Education, 1992.

_____. *The Graduation Program Working Paper: Partnerships for Learners*. Victoria: Ministry of Education, 1992.

Hagen's ministerial statement:

Hagen, Anita. "Year 2000 Update." *The Deputy's Newsletter*, May 1992.

Examples of 1992-93 media coverage of Year 2000:

Balcom, Susan. "Parents give Year 2000 a failing grade." *Vancouver Sun*, Feb. 9, 1993.

Balcom, Susan. "School children still learning the 3R's, but in a different way." *Vancouver Sun*, Feb. 18, 1993.

Nikiforuk, Andrew. "When will they ever learn?" *Western Living*, September 1993.

Quinn, Hal. "Year 2000 or bust." *Maclean's*, Jan. 11, 1993.

Smith, Charlie. "Leap of faith." *Vancouver*, June 1992.

The government's attempt to communicate the Year 2000 to the public:

British Columbia Ministry of Education. *Changes in Education: A Guide for Parents*. Victoria: Queen's Printer, 1992.

Report on the Angus Reid poll:

Southam News. "System failing, many people say." *Vancouver Sun*, Feb. 5, 1993.

Chapter 6

BCTF survey of teachers on Year 2000 techniques:

Kuehn, Larry. "Changing Teacher Practice: Teachers' Aspirations Meet School Realities." Vancouver: B.C. Teachers' Federation research department, December 1993.

Education reform:

Fullan, Michael. *The Meaning of Educational Change*. Toronto: OISE Press, 1982.

_____. *The New Meaning of Educational Change*. Toronto: OISE Press, 1991.

Leithwood, K. A., M. Holmes and D.J. Montgomery. *Helping Schools Change: Strategies Derived from Field Experience*. Toronto: Ontario Institute for Studies in Education, 1979.

Sarason, Seymour B. *The Predictable Failure of Educational Reform*. San Francisco: Jossey-Bass, 1990.

_____. *The Culture of the School and the Problem of*

Change. (second edition) Boston: Allyn & Bacon, 1982.

Ungerleider, Charles S. "Why Change (Hardly Ever) Happens," In *Dilemmas in Educational Change*. Edited by Ted Riecken and Deborah Court. Calgary: Detselig, 1993.

Werner, Walter. "Program Implementation and Experienced Time." *Alberta Journal of Educational Research*, 23 (1988): 90-108.

Education reform on a small scale:

Court, Deborah and Ted Riecken. "The Seeds of Growth and the Winds of Change: A Study of the Quality of Classroom Life in British Columbia, Part One." *Education Canada*, Winter 1991, 41-47.

_____. "The Seeds of Growth and the Winds of Change: Change and Stability, Classroom Life in British Columbia, Part Two," *Education Canada*, Spring 1992, 36-39.

Sandhu, Rob, and Ed Harrison. "Dis-ease of Implementation: Who's Responsible?" *Teacher*, April 1994.

Wideen, Marvin F. *The Struggle for Change: The Story of One School*. London: Falmer Press, 1994.

Chapter 7

Polls on education commissioned by the B.C. government:

Decima Research. "A Decima Research Report to Government of British Columbia, Ministry of Education." Unpublished document, June 1993.

_____. "Report to the British Columbia Ministry of Education on Attitudes Toward Education in the Province." Unpublished document, January 1990.

Longwoods International. "Education Issues in British Columbia." Unpublished document prepared for the B.C. Ministry of Education, May, 1992.

Synergistics Consulting Ltd. "Public Opinion Survey on Change in the Education System." Unpublished document submitted to Communications Branch, B.C. Ministry of Education, February 1991.

Documents released by the NDP in 1993 on changes to Year 2000:

B.C. Ministry of Education. *Improving the Quality of Education in British Columbia: Changes to British Columbia's Education Policy*. Victoria: Ministry of Education, November 1993.

_____. *The Intermediate Program Policy: Grades 4 to 10*. Victoria: Ministry of Education, December 1993.

_____. *The Graduation Program Policy: Grades 11 and 12*. Victoria: Ministry of Education, December 1993.

Accounts of the bureaucracy's resistance to changes in Year 2000:

Baldrey, Keith. "Dialogue 'intense,' premier says." *Vancouver Sun*, Nov. 17, 1993.

Palmer, Vaughn. "New Year 2000 just smile over substance." *Vancouver Sun*, Nov. 16, 1993.

Documents released by the NDP in 1994 on changes to Year 2000:

B.C. Ministry of Education. *The Kindergarten to Grade 12 Education Plan*. Victoria: Ministry of Education, 1994.

_____. *Implementation Resource Part 1: Guidelines for the Kindergarten to Grade 12 Education Plan*. Victoria: Ministry of Education, 1994.

_____. *Implementation Resource Part 2: Instructional Strategies and School Organization*. Victoria: Ministry of Education, 1994.

_____. *Guidelines for Student Reporting for the Kindergarten to Grade 12 Education Plan*. Victoria: Ministry of Education, 1994.

_____. *Putting Policies Into Practice Implementation Guide*. Victoria: Ministry of Education, 1994.

Reaction to the government's change in the direction of Year 2000:

Begin, Dennis. "Self-Directed Means Self-Destructive," *Teacher*, May/June 1994.

Blakeston, Judith. "Back to the Future: Education Change in B.C." *Teacher*, October 1993.

Chatterson, Dean. "A Response to the 'New' Intermediate Program." *Teacher*, May/June 1994.

Kuehn, Larry. "B.C. Teachers Support Change." *Teacher*, October 1993.

————. "Where To Now? New Directions for B.C. Education." Draft, unpublished document, Feb. 7, 1995.

Wood, Chris. "A Classroom Retreat." *Maclean's*, Dec. 6, 1993.

Chapter 8

The back-to-basics and traditional school movements:

Knickerbocker, Nancy. "Pass or Fail?" *Pacific Current*, March 1995.

Saunders, Doug. "The Irate Parent Industry." *This Magazine*, September/October 1994.

Chapter 9

Secondary schools:

Davis, Bob. "Canadian High Schools: Back to Growing Up Numb and Dumb." *Canadian Dimension*, September 1990.

Hoekter, J. and W.P. Ahlbrand. "The persistence of recitation." *American Educational Research Journal*, 6 (1969): 145-167.

King, Alan, et al. *The Teaching Experience.* Toronto: Ontario Secondary School Teachers' Federation, 1988.

Choice schools and charter schools:

No author. "Charter schools: Lessons Canada can learn," A report arising from the National Charter Schools Conference, Detroit, October, 1994. Kelowna: Teachers for Excellence in Education, 1994.

Wickstrom, Rod. "Educational Change: Can we make sense of reality?" *Education Canada*, Winter 1994.

The politics of education:

Elam, Stanley M. "Differences Between Educators and the Public on Questions of Education Policy." *Phi Delta Kappan*, December 1987, 294-296.

Hartoonian, Michael. "Good Education, Bad Politics: Practices and Principles of Reform." *Education Digest*, November 1991: 31-35.

Kaestle, Carl F. "Public Schools, Public Mood: The Pendulum Swings." *Education Digest*, November 1990: 32-35.

Kuehn, Larry. "Education in B.C.: Who Makes the Decisions?" *Legal Perspectives*, November/December 1994.

National Commission on Excellence in Education. *A Nation At Risk: The imperative for Educational Reform.* Washington: National Commission on Excellence in Education, 1983.

Scherer, Joseph J. "Education Platforms in Partisan Politics," *Education Digest*, March 1990: 51-54.

The future of B.C. education:

Grieve, Tarrance D. "Effectiveness and Efficiency in School District Governance: Keeping Students at the Centre, Putting it All Into Perspective." Notes for a paper presented at B.C. School Trustees Association conference, Dec. 9, 1994.

INDEX